GOLD LEAF,
PAINT & GLASS

GOLD LEAF, PAINT & GLASS

FRANCES FEDERER

Thomas Publications, London

© Thomas Publications 2012
20 Valonia Gardens
London SW18 1PY

Frances Federer is identified as the author of this book in
accordance with Section 77 of the Copyright, Designs and Patent Act,
1988 and asserts her moral rights.

BRITISH LIBRARY CATALOGUING IN PUBLICATION DATA
A CIP record for this book is available from The British Library

ISBN 978 0 9572694 0 8

Typeset by www.bookproductionservices.co.uk

Printed and bound in the UK by the MPG Books Group,
Bodmin and King's Lynn

☙ CONTENTS ☙

☙ FOREWORD ❧

There are, today and in the past, two basic ways of attaching gold leaf (or other pure precious metals or alloys in the form of extremely thin sheets) to the surface of glass. It can either be affixed at room temperature using an adhesive, or affixed using great heat. This book is about the former 'cold' method of application.

In processes utilising heat, there are, historically, two approaches. In the first, the decoration is temporarily glued to the cold surface of the glass, and then fired to a temperature at which the glass softens or nearly softens. Without significant wear, the gold will remain intact indefinitely. Gold and enamel decoration on Venetian glass of about the year 1500 was carried out in this way.

A second 'hot' method can be employed. The preceding process is done, followed immediately by the addition of another layer of colorless glass atop the decoration. This method results in utter permanence, as the decoration is inaccessible to harmful agents like water and is isolated from abrasion. Roman 'base-discs' of the fourth century were made in this way. These have, variously, gold leaf, enamel, or – much rarer – gilded fine glass threads elaborately flame-worked protected between their two layers of glass. Completely intact examples look nearly as the day that they were made.

Whichever of the two hot methods is used, a kiln is required capable of fine temperature control within a tremendous range: from room temperature to about 593°C (1100°F). This is essential: if the glass is heated too quickly or unevenly, the object well may crack. If the work gets too hot for too long, it will collapse under its own weight. If cooled too quickly, it will surely crack; the finished work must be carefully annealed. Today, as in Roman times, successful firing of gold (and enamel) decoration requires both highly specialized equipment and a worker with great skill and experience. All of this, it should be noted, is needed in addition to the formidable complexities of creating the decoration in the first place.

Cold decoration, not intended for firing, is a very different matter and is, perhaps surprisingly, much more challenging for the artist/craftsperson: upon completion of the gilding and painting processes, decoration intended for firing is expected to remain intact for hours or days, at most: fusion resulting from the extreme heat will give it endurance. By sharp contrast, in a cold-painting workshop when the decorator completes his or her work, their knowledge and skill alone will determine whether the decoration survives for months or for centuries.

Here is the challenge: The smooth surface of glass – its lack of 'tooth', in distinction, say, to canvas, wood, or copper – indomitably resists the 'grip' of traditional painting media and the impregnation of pigments: ordinary paint simply does not like to stick to glass. That is the bad news.

The good news is, over many centuries, clever craftspeople have invented and refined concoctions for use as painting media, along with specialized processes that will actually result in paint sticking long-term to smooth glass … no heat required.

This book, *Gold Leaf, Paint & Glass,* brings together the results of years of research by the author into archival source-material coupled with extensive trial -and-error experimentation carried out in her workshop. Such a combination of theory and practice is essential for gleaning the real meaning from the old texts. The time-tested arcane formulae have been thoroughly modernised; intricate order-sensitive processes are thoroughly explained.

Anyone practising gilding and cold-painting on glass today has to get many very complicated things 'right' if they expect their work to last really long-term: that is why this book is so very important.

William Gudenrath, Resident Advisor at The Studio of The Corning Museum of Glass

❧ INTRODUCTION ❧

Reverse painted and gilded glass has long been recognised as a versatile and practical form of decoration but its popularity has waxed and waned over the centuries. Since the early 1980s we have been experiencing a resurgence of its use: galleries, museums, shops and magazines show us decorated glass as framed art, panels set into furniture, wall coverings and as *objets d'art*. Despite this popularity, there is little practical information on the subject.

Several publications from central Europe and numbers of international exhibition catalogues (now mostly out of print) address gilding and painting on glass from a curatorial or historical point of view and many are a rich source of information. They discuss the art in great depth but it is not their intention, nor are they probably able, to explain the processes from a practitioner's point of view. In addition, as much of reverse gilding and painting stems from German-speaking countries, most of the literature is in that language. This makes it inaccessible to many readers.

Practical instruction books on gilding, in English, often have a page on *verre églomisé* (explained on pages 1–2), but the information can be inadequate. This book intends to fill that gap. It is written for students, artists, collectors, conservators, curators, interested amateurs, teachers and designers, many of whom are ready and waiting to learn more on this topic.

A definition of the art is followed by a general overview of the history of gold engraving on glass, which spans the Americas, Europe, parts of Africa and Asia. Chapter 3 is written by Simone Bretz, a freelance conservator and restorer of reverse painting on glass (see her website at www.bretz-hinterglas.com). She focuses her history on central Europe, demonstrating how methods have changed little over the centuries. Her text is supported by hitherto unpublished illustrations from the collection of the author Wolfgang Steiner.

Each chapter builds on the previous one: the historical detail puts in context the practical information. Chapter 4 covers tools, followed by a discussion of materials; chapter 6 is a fully illustrated step-by-step project, a starting point for the beginner. The next chapter expands on all processes, with recipes and supplementary information enabling readers to move on to projects of their own. Finally, common problems and safety are covered in Chapter 8.

Illustrations of work by contemporary practitioners demonstrate a variety of approaches and designs. A glossary, bibliography and suppliers' list all enable the interested reader to pursue the subject further.

The subject of fired gilding and its processes is not covered here. This book confines itself to 'cold techniques' that need no special heat source or equipment. Neither is the restoration or conservation of painted glass, painting techniques for stained glass, nor sign-writing discussed, as these are covered elsewhere in the literature.

✎ 1 ✎
PAINTING AND GILDING UNDER GLASS

Broadly speaking, reverse painting on glass may consist of any non-fired decoration that is viewed by reflected light from the opposite side of the object.[1]

The principle of reverse engraving on glass is fairly simple: gold leaf is glued to glass with gelatine dissolved in water; burnished when dry with cotton or cottonwool; scratched through with a sharpened wooden stylus to make a design and finally covered with a layer of paint (diluted with solvents) as a colour background to offset and protect the metal leaf. Processes are in reverse order to the norm: gilding is done first and background colours are applied last.

There is no need for kilns or complex machinery; a kitchen table will suffice. However, as with many apparently simple processes, there are several variations of method and subtleties of execution.

Unfired gilding and painting on glass is inherently unstable: any kind of paint or glue applied to the front of glass without firing will sooner or later separate from its substrate or support. It is for this rea-son that gilding and painting is applied to the reverse side of glass and viewed from the front.

Terminology

The terminology used to describe reverse painting and gilding on glass can be misleading. Many know the work as *verre églomisé*, or plain *églomisé*, a term to which Jean-Baptiste Glomy, 1711–1786, gave this name, first appearing in a catalogue of the Musée de Cluny in 1852. Its adoption by museums and auction houses to refer to any sort of cold painting and gilding behind glass, including the use of powdered or metal leaf of any period, became ubiquitous. Eventually, after 80 years of this blanket term, attempts to clarify the usage began.

F.S. Eden initiated the discussion in 1932:

> ...the title *verre églomisé* should not be applied to the transparent colour and foil process – older by at least 500 years than Glomy's time – but should be confined

Figure 1.1 Bruce Jackson gilding a mirror (more information at www.goldreverre.com)

Technique
Faux antiquing with oil-based paint and thinners, splattered with alcohol or meths to spread it. Water gilded with moon gold (border), 12 kt white gold (mirror) with paper grid behind the glass for guidance.

to the process of opaque painting on the under-side of glass, with colours, with or without heightening of gold, but always without a metallic background. [2]

The following year, W.B. Honey explained the origin of the label:

> The name is derived from that of one Glomy, an 18th century dealer... and... a picture framer, who introduced a fashion of surrounding a subject with a border of gilding and colour painted behind glass, and prints framed in this way, when the style had been taken up by others, were referred to in the trade as *églomisées*.[3]

In *Toute la Vérité sur le Verre Eglomisé* (*The Whole Truth about Verre Eglomisé*),[4] Paul Guth maintained that despite overuse, indeed abuse, of this term that, he said, caused offence in some quarters, it had gone from strength to strength. All attempts to ban it proved unsuccessful. He was adamant however, that the term must *never* be used to refer to engraved gold leaf combined with paint, but *only* if combined with coloured, thinned-down varnish.

> *Insistons: il entre presque toujours un vernis coloré dans ce procédé, mais jamais de peinture.*

> We insist, a coloured varnish is always used in this process, never paint.[5]

The fight to ban the expression continued. In 1979, Rudy Eswarin wrote, optimistically:

> The habitual use of the poorly considered name *verre églomisé* should be discontinued and the effort made to correct the situation. With a little attention to the matter, when catalogs [sic] are prepared for museum collections and salerooms, it will not take long.[6]

But the label survived. In 1991, Frieder Ryser provided a detailed clarification with definitions for many techniques of painting and gilding under glass.[7] Later, the catalogue for the exhibition *Glanzlichter* included an illustrated glossary for the many unfired painting and gilding procedures practised under glass.[8] Practitioners and researchers today continue to debate the use of these labels, and numerous international terms for painting and gilding under glass are in use, including the following:

English/U.S.A. *Verre églomisé, églomisé,* reverse gilding on glass, reverse painting on glass, gold engraving under glass

Dutch *Achterglasschildering*

French *Verre églomisé, fixés sous verre, peinture sous verre*

German *Hinterglasmalerei, Eglomisé, Zwischengoldglass, Amelierung, Goldradierung*

Italian *Pittura su vetro, vetri dipinti, vetri dorati graffit, agglomizzato, fondo d'oro*

Polish *Eglomisé, malarstwo na szkle*

Czech *Hinterglasmalerei, podmalba na skle, zwischengoldglass, dvojst nné sklo*

Few of these labels carry precise meanings, but in Chapter 3 Simone Bretz defines many of them, including *églomisé,* according to recent research. Throughout this book I refer to the practice as 'gold engraving'.

Figure 1.2 Jane Richardson Mack *The Return of Don Mono,* size 46 x 36 cm (18 x14 in.)

Technique
Layered water gilding with silver leaf.
Découpage with found imagery.
Reproduction of artist's monkey portrait.

2

THE DEVELOPMENT OF GOLD ENGRAVING

Early origins

Stained glass, as a fundamental element of medieval cathedrals, depended on transmitted light for its full effect. With the increasing availability of clear glass, both coloured and colourless, its use as a decorative element within the building flourished. It was found that by decorating the back and then blocking the light from passing through, imagery could be viewed by reflected light from the front, through its supporting layer of glass. Once framed, the decoration was protected.

At first, painted foil was attached to the glass, but different methods evolved, such as:

* gluing foil directly onto the glass, removing it by scratching or engraving, then covering it with paint;
* painting the glass first, engraving the paint and then backing the whole area with foil.

By the time the Italian artist Cennino Cennini came to write his treatise, published as *Il Libro dell' Arte* (*The Craftsman's Handbook*), written around 1390, cold gilding with painting on glass was well established as a form of decoration.[9]

Gutenberg's printing press marked a huge advance. The spread of vast numbers of copperplate engravings in the late Renaissance, reproducing the latest studio paintings, gave craftsmen far and wide access to any number of compositions suitable for reproduction on glass. The most inventive painters mixed and matched prints to make unique compositions of their own. Wolfgang Steiner has made a study of glass paintings, matching them with the engravings that were their sources of origin.[10]

The ravaging Thirty Years War, 1618-48, left Switzerland relatively unscathed and Zürich continued as a hub for reverse painting on glass, or *Hinterglasmalerei*, as it was known. At one time this small city supported over 20 practitioners of the art, but

Figure 2.1 *The Penitent St Mary Magdalen*, 1660–75, Courtesy Victoria and Albert Museum, London. no. 146–1879.

Technique
Picture: water gilding, engraved .
Painted with red, blue and green oil-based lacquers and blue opaque paint (*amelierung*), backed with silvery foil.
Frame: water gilding, engraved, oil-based paint.

the war had its effect. Painters left Zürich in part to extend their experience, but also to seek new patronage. One destination was Naples, ruled by the Spanish branch of the Hapsburg Empire. A number of talented Neapolitan painters, influenced by the incoming Swiss, adopted their techniques while raising the art to new levels of skill.[11]

The spread of glass decoration through Europe

By the 1670s, French intolerance of the Huguenot Protestants in their midst forced the exile of many highly trained craftsmen. Coincidentally, skilled Venetian glass makers, bound to secrecy, were also making their escape and Great Britain became the beneficiary of a wave of expertise in glass manufacture and decoration. The widespread construction of great houses for the ruling classes ensured work for the émigrés. Looking-glasses, known today as mirrors, of massive proportions were enlarged even further with borders of ornamental glass. Under the influence of the designer Daniel Marot,[12] French émigrés who were trained engravers adapted their skills to engraving gold on glass.

Engraved gold was backed with solid colours of blue or green for bedrooms, black for mourning, or a translucent red lacquer. This last was further backed, or covered, with foil, such as tin. This was the *amelierung* technique described in detail in the next chapter. Looking-glasses in this style were also made in France and Sweden, but the practice of such labour- intensive methods, was as ever, short-lived. By 1700 the style was over.

Zwischengoldglas, 'between gold glass' or 'sandwich gold glass', was a process whereby engraved water

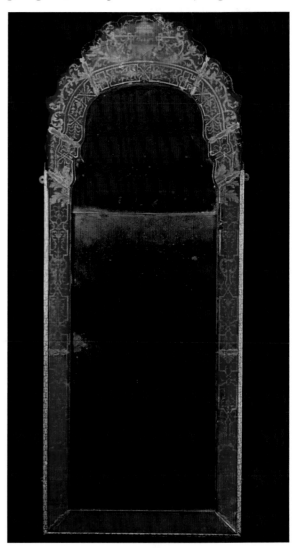

Figure 2.3 Pier glass c. 1690–1700, 164 x 65 cm (64½ x 25½ in.)

Figure 2.2 Engraving by Jean Bérain.[13]

Figure 2.4 detail of Fig. 2.3.

Technique
Amelierung
Water gilding, engraved.
Painted with oil-based red lacquer.
Backed with silvery foil.

Figure 2.5 Beaker with *Singerie* motif. Germany, probably Saxony, 1720–30, Victoria and Albert Museum, London, no. 8957. About 8 cm (3 in.) tall.

Technique (unknown but speculated)
Two glasses blown, ground and polished to fit exactly within one another.
Glass 1, outer. Inside: water gilded, engraved (upside down and in reverse). All extra gold removed. Painted overall in *faux* agate, with oil-based paints.
Glass 2, inner. Outside: water gilded. Maybe protected with a varnish of some kind.
The two are assembled and sealed at the rim with a resin. The glass would have been usable as a vessel.

gilding was sandwiched between two layers of closely fitting glass. This was a painstaking, time-consuming and infinitely more risky undertaking than border panels for looking-glasses. The system involved gilding and engraving the outer surface of one vessel, fitting a slightly larger vessel over it and sealing the two to render the object impermeable to water. Teams of skilled craftsmen carried out the work, blowing, cutting, grinding, polishing, gilding, engraving, painting and finally gluing. It was practiced mainly in Bohemia (an area that is now part of the Czech Republic) and in Saxony (Germany) where most of the marbled glass, as in Fig. 2.5, was made.

Mass production

Within a relatively short space of time, the production of painted glass panels developed from small cottage industries into substantial businesses in the

Figure 2. 6 *St Georgius*, Noder Workshop, Seehausen/ Staffelsee (Germany), 2nd quarter 19th century, glass size: 25.2 x 18.6 cm (10 x 7 in.). HGS 123.[15]

Technique
Outline traced in black paint.
Painted with oil-based paint and powdered gold paint.

mountainous and forested areas of central Europe, such as Alsace, Bavaria, Bohemia and Romania.

Several factors could explain this:

* harsh weather conditions prevented travel while the fear of contagious disease further isolated communities;
* offcuts of glass, possibly cheaper than paper, would have been plentiful from the many local glass factories;
* a long-established tradition of furniture making (for frames) and painted folk art already existed.

Catholic faith in those regions ensured a demand for icons painted on glass; it was believed pictures of favourite saints would protect their homes. Production steadily increased. In Sandl, Austria, the output of a single family workshop reached an astonishing 386,000 reverse glass paintings within 12 years.[14] By the early 19th century it had reached its peak.

The Americas, N. Africa and East Asia

From remote mountainous regions all over Europe framed, painted glass panels were transported by foot over the mountains by *kraxenmänner* (*kraxe*: framed rucksack) – men with specially constructed baskets which extended over their heads, strapped to their backs. From Cadiz in Spain, the glass was shipped west to North America and the West Indies, south to north Africa and east to India, Persia, the East Indies and East Asia. In time, painters in Spain, Italy, the United States, China, Senegal, India and Thailand began to produce their own glass painting based on existing local traditions. In French-speaking Senegal, 'Suwer painting' is widely practised today.

There is more information at www.senegal-online.com/anglais/galeries/sous-verre.

Once Jesuit missionaries had taught the Chinese how to paint with oils, a thriving import/export business in glass painting began. Mirrored glass, exported from Britain to China specifically for the purpose, had sections of silvering scraped away to be replaced with exquisite reverse-painted portraits and domestic scenes, rendered in western style for the European market.[16] Back in the west, the panels were reframed with contemporary carved giltwood (gilded wood). The true provenance of this work escaped the notice of many western collectors and dealers who believed much of it to be authentically European – *plus ça change*.[17] The Chinese domestic market, meanwhile, enjoyed finely painted erotica on glass.

In Britain and the United States, demand grew for gilded and painted glass panels inserted into furniture, such as mirror frames, known as overmantels, *bureaux* and clock cases.

British overmantels tended to be of modest size: indeed, at times were very small and dainty. The glass friezes of the smallest were decorated by transferring copperplate engravings and hand colouring them. Known as English Glass Pictures, they are recognisable by their yellowish, patinated discolouration and faded colours. The subjects were commonly portraits. For medium to large overmantels, the pro-

Figure 2.7 Courtesy M. Groot. Example of Suwer painting, Senegal. Made between 1920 and 1930. Size 42.5 x 41cm (1 ft 4 x 1 ft 3 in.). No signature.

Technique
Applied photograph c. 1920.
Painting made with oil-based paints, possibly house paints.

Figure 2.8 Panel depicting Charlotte at Werther's tomb, a famous scene from the novel, *Die Leiden des Jungen Werthers* or *The Sorrows of Young Werther* by Goethe. The novel, published in 1774, recounts an unhappy romantic infatuation that came to unfortunate end, and was a very popular design motif for a period after the book was published. Signed and dated. L.Phillips, 1792, size: 142 x 69 cm (56 x 29 in.) Courtesy Apter-Fredericks Ltd., Ref. 46288.

Technique
Water gilding, engraved.
Backed with asphaltum (see Chapter 5 page 31).
Excess leaf removed.
Backed with coloured gesso (see page 30).

duction of hand-made gilded glass panels increased quickly. Paintings, usually of pastoral scenes often with ornate borders, were carried out swiftly and to formula. Across the Atlantic, proportions could be generous and decoration ornate. The birth of a new nation generated copious rising phoenixes and presidential portraits. The largest overmantels included multiple glass panels let into the top, sides and base. But, once again, the accountants stepped in. Hand painting was forced to give way to cheaper mass-produced gilded cast plaster and composition friezes. The genre had lasted scarcely thirty years.

Folk art painted on glass similarly faced pressure from industry. Increasing competition from photography and high-quality colour printing nearly put an end to it. But it did not completely die out. In the summer of 1908, a small party of walkers in Bavaria discovered the village of Murnau, which was a glass-painting centre. The walkers were Gabriele Münter, her lover Wassily Kandinsky and some of their friends, all members of the Blue Rider group of painters, and at Murnau they met one of the last remaining members of a glass-painting family. The group was enchanted not only by the landscape but with the depth of colour and artistic potential of painting on glass. The next year Münter bought a home in Murnau and the group settled there, living and working together in what was known as The Russian House. The painters produced large numbers of works on canvas and on glass, experimenting with the new medium.

The 20th century to today

The early years of the 20th century also brought a new awareness of the commercial potential of decorated glass.

In the United States, the use of gilded and painted glass panels was principally for sign-writing purposes and reflected the needs of an increasingly prosperous society. At the height of their popularity, fairgrounds, the breweries and railways all utilised glass for decoration and advertising purposes, an extravagance almost brought to an end by Prohibition in the 1920s and the Depression a decade later. Commercial sign-writing on glass continues today, displaying a variety of baroque practices in spite of, or as a result of, computer technology. It rarely, if ever, includes engraving, though.

Gilded glass has experienced a resurgence of popularity as a decorative feature for interiors in the last ten to twenty years. Painting and gilding, using methods almost unchanged since the Renaissance, is today applied to any kind of clear or even coloured glass for jewellery, pictures, wall coverings and as panels set into furniture, for example screens and tabletops.

From the 12th century on, treatises on gilding on glass describe methods from fusing sandwich glass, with its filling of cut-out gold foil, to gluing gold leaf down with beaten egg white. The following chapter traces the history of such techniques drawn from contemporaneous literature and includes recipes demonstrating the continuity of methods through the centuries.

Figure 2.9 French border glass, signed by Hoeth of Lyon. Date unknown.

Technique
Paint applied over a stencil.
Engraved through paint for signature, only
Water gilding.
Painted with oil-based paints.

Figure 2.10 David A. Smith 'Whittaker' sign, 91.5 x 116.8 cm (36 x 46 in.).

Techniques
Multiple, from brilliant glass cutting to water gilding and painting. See www.davidadriansmith.com.

Figure 2.12 Peter Binnington, detail of one of a set of matching furniture. Design, Linley.

Technique
Crumpled aluminium foil placed behind blue glass.

Figure 2.11 Frances Federer, necklace.

Technique
Engraved water gilding.
Matt gilding with coloured leaf.
Varnish, mounted in silver.

Figure 2.13 Frances Federer, free-standing screen, 170 x 165 cm (5.7 x 5.5 in.).

Technique
Water gilded with a variety of leaf.
Oil-based paint.

3

HISTORIC SOURCES AND RECIPES
by Simone Bretz

To an artist painting under glass, a number of choices and challenges present themselves. Which metal leaf, glue, design and method of back-up to use, and how do the various media react with one another? The question of durability arises: if the decoration is not fired, how can these processes, applied to a smooth, vitreous surface, be made to last? What is the best choice of materials and techniques?

Methods, ingredients and tools used for decorating glass have been documented in treatises and recipe books since the Middle Ages. A continuous thread of technique has changed little over the centuries.

This chapter looks at what can be learned from the past. The recipes reproduced here are in their original, or translated forms. Though they can be a little vague in early books, as in any trade gilders have their own preferred ways and recipes may vary. For example, a recipe for glair may include the addition of water in one treatise but not in another. The principles of sticking gold leaf on to glass, whether subsequently fired or not, have, however, largely remained consistent over the centuries.

The illustrations have been carefully chosen to support the text and illustrate the methods under discussion. Unless otherwise indicated all are from the Wolfgang Steiner Collection.

Antiquity

The earliest surviving examples of reverse-painted glass include a rock crystal plate from 1500 BC (now in the Heraklion Museum, Crete) and a small glass depicting a sphinx from Mesopotamia, dated 800 BC.[18]

Reverse-decorated glass was practised in various parts of the Roman Empire, between the first and third centuries AD. in Rome, Syria and other Middle Eastern countries. To mark graves, it was customary to break off the bases of free-blown bowls and beakers, which carried decoration of Jewish and Christian motifs and embed them in the plastered walls of Roman catacombs.[19] The method of decoration used, gold foil 'heat-sealed' between two layers of glass, is known as *fondi d'oro*. It was difficult work, probably demanding more from the glass technician than from the artist.

The Benedictine monk Theophilus, author of *De diversis artibus* (published c. 1125), describes the *fondi d'oro* technique fully in Chapter XIII of the second book. The sandwich of two layers of glass, with a filling of gold and/or silver foil, had to be fused in the furnace without rolling up or blackening the metal. There could be no air bubbles trapped within the sandwich, nor must the two layers of glass separate nor shatter on cooling. Care also had to be taken not to melt the foil; silver melts above 960°C (1760°F) and gold melts above 1060°C (1950°F). If the kiln temperature rises above this, the foil would be destroyed.

XIII. Glass goblets which the Byzantines embellish with gold and silver.

The Byzantines also make costly drinking goblets out of the same blue stones, embellishing them with gold in this way. They take gold leaf, about which we spoke above, and from it shape representations of men, birds, animals, or foliage. Then they apply these on the goblet with water, in whatever place they have selected. This gold leaf must be rather thick. Then they take glass that is very clear, like crystal, which they make up themselves and which melts soon after it feels the heat of the fire. They grind it carefully on a porphyry stone with water and apply it very thinly all over the gold leaf with a brush. When it is dry, they put (the goblet) in the kiln in which painted glass for windows is fired and about which we shall speak later. Underneath they light a fire of beechwood that has been thoroughly fired in smoke; and when they have seen the flame penetrating the goblet long enough for it to take on a slight reddening, they immediately throw out the wood and block up the kiln until it cools by itself. This gold will never come off.[20]

The early Middle Ages

The earliest source of cold gilding is the *Lucca Manuscript*, 800 AD, so named after the mid-Italian town of its origin. A Greek author discusses dyeing wood and bone, gilding on glass, the preparation of paints and the treatment of metals. He suggests egg white as a mordant for gold. 'Mordant' in this context means glue and 'glair' refers only to egg white.

> For whatever kind of gilding always use a binding medium from a hen's egg, also for gilding on glass the same serves.[21]

14th–15th centuries in Italy

Mary P. Merrifield (1804–1889) was an historian and translator of early paint techniques. Thanks to her attention to detail, many traditional methods and recipes have been passed down to us, for example a description of the manufacture of sandwich gold glass. In her translation of the *Bolognese Treatise*, a recipe book from Northern Italy of the mid-15th century, Alexandrian borax was specified as a bond to fix metal foil onto glass. Pulverised borax (sodium borate which appears in crystalline form when salt lakes dry out) mixed with water, was applied to a sheet of glass and the gold laid on to it. The gilded sheet was fired at a temperature of about 880°C (1616°F). A second, hot sheet of glass was then placed over the foil as a protective layer and the whole sandwich fused.

To lay gold upon glass.

Take very thin bladders of crystal glass, as clean and pure, and liquid as possible and break them just as you please, and lay real gold upon them. And Frate Giovanni told me that in order to fix the gold on to the glass, it was necessary to employ a solution of borax, the Alexandrian borax, which the goldsmiths use, for this water makes the gold adhere well. And when you have laid the gold on to the white glass, put it in the mouth of the furnace, that is, where you stand to work, so that it may become hot, and take care as it dries to have ready in the furnace the glass upon which you wish to lay the gold, and with this glass some fine saffron of Mars of the alchemists must be mixed, in order to serve as a mordant for the gold, which will appear of a deeper colour. Then take out of the furnace the quantity of glass which you require, and heat it upon the marble slab upon which you make drinking glasses, and be quick, and take it with the iron for making drinking glasses, and lay upon it the piece covered with gold, and put the gold on the under side of it, that is, let it between the two glasses. Then put it in the furnace to spread, and spread the glass with the gold in it with another iron, and when you see that it is well spread out and that it adheres well together, take it out and set it to cool on the top, where you set the rest of the glass to cool, and then use it for your purpose just as you please.[22]

Sometimes, black or dark blue glass was used as the supporting panel, giving colour to the gold and avoiding the need for paint.

Another recipe for gilding with borax in a kiln was found in a 17th-century manuscript:

XI To gild glass that will melt.

Dissolve borax in water / with this mixture paint the glass in your way / gild the glass/ in the case of a drinking vessel / fill with salt and set in a kiln / heat to a suitable temperature/ this will fix the borax on the glass forever. This is one of the most beautiful ways of gilding.[23]

Figure 3.1 Fondo d'oro, Byzantium, 8th -10th century, size: 4.8 x 4.6 cm (1⅞ x 1¾ in). HGS 603

Technique
Black base glass panel decorated with cut out and punched gold foil.
Covered with clear glass layer and fused.

Most reverse-gilded glass engravings produced during the Renaissance originated from areas of northern Italy, notably Padua, Florence and Siena, where the Italian masters had access to panels of colourless glass.[24] The earliest known, reliable instructions for metal foil engraving on glass were published in *Il Libro dell' Arte* by the artist Cennino Cennini (referred to in Chapter 2). Drawing on established traditions, Cennini describes the preparation of glass and size for gilding. He goes on to explain the process of gilding, which tools to use and methods for backing up with oil paint.

CLXXII How to gild glass for reliquary ornaments.

There is another process for working on glass, indescribably attractive, fine and unusual, and this is a branch of great piety, for the embellishment of holy reliquaries; and it calls for sure and ready draftsman-

ship. This process is carried out as follows. Take a piece of white glass, with no green cast, very clean, free from bubbles; and wash it, rubbing it down with lye and charcoal. And rinse it with good clear water, and let it dry by itself. But before you wash it, cut it in such a four-side form, whatever you like to get. Whisk the white of a fresh egg with a stick, so that it is thoroughly beaten; and let it distill overnight. Then take a minever brush, and with this brush wet the back of the glass with this glair; and when it is thoroughly wet all over, take a leaf of the gold, which should be quite heavy gold, that is, dull; put it on the paper tip, and lay it deftly on the glass where you have wet it; and press it down with a little very clean cotton, gently, so that the glair does not get on top of the gold; and lay the whole glass in this way. Let it dry without sun for the space of some days.

CLXXII Arrangements for drawing on this glass.

When it is all dry, get a nice flat little panel, covered with black cloth or silk; and have a little study of your own, where no one will cause you any sort of interruption, and which has just one cloth covered window; and you will put your table in this window, as if for writing, so arranged that the light shines over your head when you have your face turned toward this window. With your glass laid out on this black cloth.

CLXXII How to draw on the gilded glass.

Take a needle, fastened in a little stick as if it were a little brush, and have it quite sharp pointed. And, with the name of God, begin to draw lightly with this needle whatever figure you wish to make. And have this first drawing show very little, for it can never be erased; and therefore work lightly until you get your drawing settled; then proceed to work as if you were sketching with a pen, for this work has to be done freehand. And do you want to be convinced that you need to have a light hand, and that it should not be tired? [Know] that the strongest shadow you can make consists in penetrating to the glass with the point of the needle, and no more; that the intermediate shadow consists in not piercing through the gold all over; that it is as delicate as that, and you must not work with haste—rather with great enjoyment and pleasure. And I give you this advice, that the day before the day you want to work at this job, you hold your hand to your neck, or in your bosom, so as to get it all unburdened of blood and weariness.

CLXXII How to scrape the gold off the backgrounds.

When you have got your drawing finished, and you want to scrape away certain grounds, which generally want to be put in with ultramarine blue in oil, take a leaden style, and rub the gold, which it takes off for you neatly; and work carefully around the outlines of the figure.

CLXXII How to back up the drawing with colours.

Take various colours ground in oil, such as ultramarine blue, black, verdigris, and lac; and if you want any drapery or lining to glisten [in lines of gold] on green, apply green; if you want it on lac, apply lac; if you want it on black, apply black. But the black is the most striking of all, for it shows up the figures better than any other colour.[25]

Around 1500, a change occurred in the general character of reverse gilding and painting on glass. Originally used for domestic altars, the demand for luxury goods widened its applications to painted and gilded jewellery, medallions, rosaries and amulets. Small reverse paintings in muted colours, usually on carved rock crystal, were produced in Lombardy until the end of the 16th century.[26]

A recipe for oil gilding was found in *Secreti Diversi*, a manuscript from the Marciana library in Venice, dating from the beginning to mid-16th century. This treatise is a medical book, but it includes recipes for varnishing and the preparation of paint.

Mordant for gilding glass, which has been tried by a Venetian friar.

Take one ounce of mastic which has been roasted, not burnt, but dried carefully, one ounce of coperosa which must be fine and white and not grey, one ounce of varnish in grains, and half one ounce of burnt roche alum. Pulverise the ingredients finely, and grind them up with well-purified linseed oil. When you use this mordant, grind it with linseed oil well purified, and when you use it distemper it with the same oil, so that it may be of the consistence of ink, lay it on the glass, and expose it to the sun when it does not shine very

strongly, and if the sun is very hot, place it in the shade, but in such a place that the sun may reflected on it, and let it dry so far that when touched with the finger a slight impression may left on it. When this is the case, lay on the gold and let it dry well; then clean it with cotton, varnish the gold, and let it become perfectly dry. But do not wash vases gilded in this manner except with fresh water, and be very careful in rubbing them.[27]

14th–15th centuries in Burgundy, Flanders and the Lower Rhine

In the years preceding the outbreak of the Thirty Years' War in 1618, several highly skilled stained glass artists in Burgundy, Flanders and the Lower Rhine also painted on the underside of glass. The paint, black enamel (using metal oxide), was the same as for stained glass but left unfired.[28] A dark outline was followed with *grisaille*, washes of the same paint to create tones, and this was followed by opaque paint of various colours. Some areas were covered with beaten gold, silver or tin. Assembling smaller panels and framing them together in lead created larger works.

16th–17th centuries in South Germany and Switzerland

In Nurnberg, several workshops practiced the new style of reverse painted glass. The designations *amelieren, amolieren, amulieren* and *gamalieren* were found by Frieder Ryser in several 16th- and 17th- century German documents; the first reference to reverse engraving specifically was made in 1532.[29] This term is close to the term *emailieren*, which means enamelling, fired enamels, but they should not be confused. The technique now known as *amelierung* was used to produce decorative panels for cabinets, backgammon sets, beakers, caskets, decorative mirrors, rings and thimbles.[30] It reached its highest point in Switzerland at the beginning of the 17th century where it was used to imitate precious tableware and textiles like brocade.

Figure 3.2 Bird Ornament, South Germany, about 1600, glass size: c. 9.5 x 11.5 cm (3¾ x 4½ in.). HGS.

Technique
Amelierung
Applied gold leaf, engraved.
Painted with red, blue and green lacquers and blue opaque paint.
Backed with tin foil.

To produce a glass panel decorated with *amelierung*, metal leaf or metal powder as a paint was applied to clear glass and then engraved. Translucent lacquers (lustres) were then painted over the engraving. These lustres were made from resin or an oil/resin mixture with transparent pigments, such as yellow, orange, red, brown, green, blue and purple, added. Placing crumpled tin or silver foil over the lustres as a third layer added luminosity. Instead of painted glass absorbing light, beaten metal reflected it back. The process imitated light transmitted through a coloured stained-glass window.

As has been mentioned, *amelierung* flourished in Switzerland and Hans Jakob Sprüngli (1559–1637) was one of the most important stained-glass painters in the Zürich area. He collaborated with the finest goldsmiths using these processes to make tankards and double-walled bowls, besides undertaking commissions from emperors and princes for framed glass panels to add to their treasure collections.

A treatise by Matthäus Merian, translated by Thomas Garzoni in *Piazza Universale* in 1641, describes the method.

> There is yet another glass painting technique known as *Amelieren* which is made with paint out of mastic/turpentine and other materials, paint behind the glass without heat, in particular on drinking dishes, bowls and such like, and it looks lovely and beautiful.[31]

Figure 3.3 *Reclining Venus with Cupid*, Hans Jakob Sprüngli, Zürich, about 1610-1620, size: height 11.5 cm (4½ in), diameter 21.4 cm (8½ in). Schlossmuseum, Collection of Applied Art, Foundation Schloss Friedenstein Gotha, K 347.

Technique
Applied gold leaf, engraved.
Painted parchment glued to glass, *faux* reverse glass painting (figures).
Painted with orange, red, blue and green lacquers and backed with tin foil (*amelierung*).
Painted with opaque paint.

It is very likely that Sprüngli wrote the recipe chapters that appeared in Johannes Kunckel's 1689 *Ars vitraria experimentalis*, ending with the initials H.I.S.[32] Creating a double-walled beaker is described in recipe XXVII as 'a peculiar curious drinking glass to make'.[33] Here are some of his recipes.

About glass gilding and painting

XI All kinds of grounds for gold on glass.

Take gum Arabic, put in a good wine vinegar, which has been filtered through paper, leave it to stand a while so it will become as white as flour, then pour the vinegar off and rub the gum on a stone with a little fresh and pure amygdalorum gum, which is gum from the almond tree (you can also use cherry tree gum if it is clean) and a little clear water, paint what you want on the glass with your pleasure, and as it will be almost dry, so that it will be a little tacky, lay the gold on it, so it will be, where you have done right, the gold fully shine through the glass. Remove the excess of gold, after it has entirely dried over a moderate coal fire, mildly with cotton wool, (but hold the glass far from the coals, so that it does not shatter), so the gold will be appear very beautifully on the glass, and never, if it would get wet from water or such, it will come off or be defaced.

XII Another glass-gold-ground.

Take a little powdered mastic, let it dissolve in gum-water over a moderate heat, so that it has consistency of a varnish; paint or coat the glass, lay afterwards on it the beaten gold or silver or metal, and leave to dry completely by a coal fire and moderate warmth.

XIII Yet another ground for gilding.

Take *Silberglett* [silver oxide], grind it dry first on a stone, till fine as flour; after this grind it, with clear turpentine varnish, coat therewith by a soft deer brush, leave it to dry like other gold-grounds, but that it remains slightly tacky, apply afterwards the gold, and press it with cotton wool, leave it till quite dry, and the wipe the rest smoothly off.

XXIV A special gilding.

Take an egg, put the white in a glass or beaker, beat completely to a foam; leave to stand, so clear water forms below. Take that water, add a little saffron to it and write with that; cut the silver or gold to tiny pieces, wide enough to cover the lines or the letters, lay it on the writing, while it is yet wet, leave to dry; then take cotton wool, burnish over the gold writing, so to get rid of the left over, that is not written; but if it should glow more, polish with a tooth.

In the H.I.S. treatise there is information about engraving in gold.

> …lay the gold on it, leave to dry, engrave it to your taste, one can draw and engrave beautiful figures into it.[34]

Jacobus Bornitius was a little more precise about *amelierung* and contributed this, in 1625:

> *Amelieren* is a painting [technique] by which gilded glass with a pen is engraved. It needs a steady and not shaky hand.[35]

Pictoria Sculptoria et quae subalternarum atrium, was written by Théodore Turquet de Mayerne, born in Switzerland in 1573. Despite his appointment as physician to the English and French monarchy, he found time to chronicle the process of gilding on the *front* of the glass as opposed to behind it.

> Gilding on a drinking glass.

> If you want to write lines or letters on a drinking glass, or gilding, take a nut shell full of linseed oil and 3 drops varnish, a 3-pea sized heap of ground mastic, a bullet of lead white and same quantity of yellow lead [like Massicot], grind all together, write or paint onto a glass, when almost dry apply gold on it; what is not written wipes off with cotton wool, but the glass must be cleaned before so that the gold is not applied to the surrounding.[36]

16th–17th centuries in Italy

The over-sized, thick dishes and bowls made at this period were works of art that suddenly appeared in the Austrian Tyrol and North Italy (Venetia), and in great numbers, without a recognisable earlier phase of development. Their long period of production ended just as abruptly. The painting was different in style and execution from the objects described above, with the quality varying greatly. They are between 3 and 4 mm (less than ¼ in.) thick and were often formed individually in the mould-cast glass technique rather than cut from larger panels. Many have irregular edges, uneven surfaces and air bubbles. Several techniques, processes now familiar to us, were combined on a single panel: the drawing

Figure 3.4 *Deposition from the Cross*, Venetian Tyrol, about 1550, glass size: 34 x 33 cm (13¼ x 12 in.). HGS 553.

Technique
Painted black outlines and black paint in different shades, backed with gold leaf (*églomisé*).
Painted with opaque paint.

Figure 3.5 *Deposition from the Cross*, chiaroscuro woodcut by Ugo da Carpi (Capri 1480-1532 Rome), after drawing by Raphael (1483–1520). HGS 553.

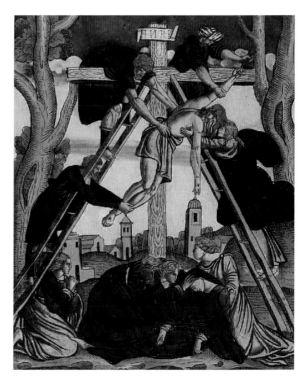

Figure 3.6 *Deposition from the Cross*, Venetian Tyrol, about 1550, glass size: 24 x 19 cm (9 x 7 in.). HGS 570.

Technique
Painted black outlines and black paint in different shades, backed with gold leaf (*églomisé*).
Painted red lacquer, backed with gold leaf and blue lacquer, backed with silver leaf (*églomisé*).
Painted with opaque paint.

outlined in black; colours filled in with a combination of opaque paint and transparent lacquers; beaten metal placed behind translucent areas to reflect light.

In Naples, the export of elaborate caskets and cabinets continued until the mid-17th century. Comprising precious materials such as ebony, ivory and tortoiseshell, often fitted with gilded bronze mounts, they also included panels of reverse glass paintings. To fit into the fronts of cabinet drawers, the glass was necessarily of small size, gaining value as miniatures in their own right and richly rewarding the artists. Swiss painters started to create their own glass panels, decorated with gold engraving or with *amelierung* technique and opaque paint.

Figure 3.7 *Coastal Landscape*, Master V.B.L., initials V.B.L., Zürich, 1st half 17th century, glass size: 9.5 x 14.5 cm (3¾ x 5¾ in.). HGS 485.

Technique
Applied gold leaf, engraved.
Backed with black paint.

Figure 3.8 *Banishment*, probably VBL workshop, Switzerland or Italy, Naples, about 1630-1660, glass size: 10.9 x 16 cm (4 x 6¼ in.). HGS 547.

Technique
Decorated with gold powder and engraved gold leaf.
Covered with orange and green lacquers.
Backed with tin foil and brass foil (*amelierung* – see image from reverse side with cardboard backing).
Painted with semi-opaque and opaque paint.

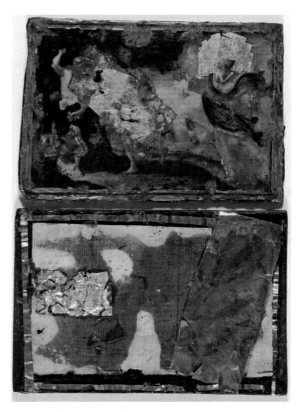

Figure 3.9 Reverse of *Banishment*, HGS 547.

Figure 3.10 *Banishment*, print by Johann Sadeler (Brussels 1550 – Venice 1600). HGS 547.

18th century

A technique that developed in the Netherlands during the 16th and 17th centuries and was also practised in Bohemia and Austria in the early 18th century came later to be defined as *églomisé*.[37] In this case it was the paint that was engraved, not the gold. A layer of gold covered the paint.

In the 18th century, on these reverse-painted glass panels the colours were reduced to brown or black paint, backed with gold.

Figure 3.13 *Death Dance – The Capitular*, probably workshop Daniel and Ignaz Preissler, Kunstat (East Bohemia), 1st half 18th century, glass size: 14.8 x 13.2 cm (5 x 5 in.). HGS 477.

Technique
Eglomisé
Painted with brown translucent paint in different shades, partially engraved.
Backed with gold leaf.

Figure 3.11 *Maundy*, Gerhard Janssen, initials G. J., Vienna, about 1700, glass size: 25.2 x 29.3 cm (10 x 11½ in). HGS 377.

Technique
Eglomisé
Painted with brown translucent paint in different shades, partially engraved.
Backed with gold leaf.

Figure 12 *Maundy*, Copper print by Wolfgang Kilian (Augsburg 1581–1662), after a pattern by Christoph Schwarz (about 1548–1592 Munich). HGS 377.

Figure 3.14 *Death Dance – The Capitular*, Copper print by Michael Rentz (Nürnberg 1701–1758 Kukus). 1741 HGS 477.

Figure 3.15 *Light Cannon*, North Bohemia/Silesia, probably Daniel Preissler (Kronstadt 1636–1733), about 1700, glass size: 16.5 x 23.3 cm (6 x 9 in.). HGS 480.

Technique
Eglomisé
Painted with black paint, engraved.
Backed with gold leaf.

Figure 3.16 *Hunter* (*Windhetzer*), Jonas Zeuner (Kassel 1727–1814 Amsterdam), signed 'Zeuner inv.', Netherlands, 2nd half 18th century, glass size: 32 x 26 cm (12½ x 10 in.). HGS 337.

Technique
Gold and silver engraving.
Applied gold and silver leaf, engraved.
Backed with black paint.

Figure 3.17 *Hunter (Windhetzer – Chasseur Aux Levrieres)*, copper print by Johann Elias Ridinger (Ulm 1698 – Augsburg 1767). HGS. 337.

Figure 3.18 *Declaration of Love*, Niklaus Michael Spengler (Konstanz 1700-1776 Darmstadt), signed and dated 'Nicol Michael/Spengler, pinx.1758.', glass size: 41.5 x 33.3 cm (16 x 13 in.). HGS 455.

Technique
Painted with red, orange, blue and green lacquers, backed with silver leaf (*églomisé*).
Painted with semi-opaque and opaque paint.

In 1719, the manual *Der Wohlanführende Mahler, The Leading or Vanguard Painter*, by Johann Melchior Cröker, appeared in Germany. In Chapter 31, it describes how to make and apply colours with lavender oil, engrave through them and how to use clear lavender oil or varnish as an oil size for the final leaf.

> All kinds of writing, flowers, and paintings to paint on glass.

> One can paint onto the glass with all kinds of colourful paints prepared with lavender oil, namely first prepare the glass followed by the application of paint, the highlights will be engraved into the paint, even with wide scratches with an engraving needle, and this will be done till the highlights are finished, and the engraved glass will be coated thinly with a clear lavender oil or varnish, left to dry, and the silver and gold will be applied.[38]

Figure 3.19 *Declaration of Love*, copperprint by Charles Joseph Flipart (Paris 1721 – Madrid 1789), after a painting by Pietro Longhi (Venice 1702–1785). HGS 455.

Figure 3.21 Detail, *Allegory of Asia*, HGS 585.

Figure 3.20 *Allegory of Asia*, Winklarn (Upper Palatinate, Germany), about 1800, glass size: 34.4 x 22 cm (13½ x 8½ in.). HGS 585.

Technique
Painted with red lacquers, backed with silver leaf – green lacquer with gold leaf (*églomisé*).
Painted with semi- opaque and opaque paint, gold and silver powder.

Figure 3.22 Reverse, *Allegory of Asia*, HGS 585.

Another popular style of glass painting of this period was to create silhouettes on glass with gold engraving, backed with black paint. *Instruction on How to Produce Silhouettes on Gold Behind Glass* by Philipp Jakob Bieling, 1791, describes not only the use of the tongue as a wetting agent (saliva) but reminds us to be sober at work.

> Moisten the absolutely clean glass with the tongue and apply the gold immediately, as soon as one can. With the smallest amount of pressure, let the gold fly on. It is necessary to remember that one needs to work sober.[39]

Figure 3.23 *Silhouettes of a Couple*, South Germany, 1793, glass size: about 17 x 10.5 cm (6¾ x 4 in.). HGS 503. 504.

Technique
Applied gold, engraved.
Backed with black paint (for portrait).
Backed with black wax (for surrounded decoration).
Covered with pink silk (visible because of loss of paint).

From about 1750 onwards, many reverse paintings on glass originated from the city of Augsburg in Southern Germany. Their influence spread to other regions in Bavaria, such as Staffelsee and Murnau. There are also gold and silver engraved glass pictures from this period; Paul von Stetten wrote in the *Kunst-Gewerbe- und Handswerks-Geschichte der Reichs-Stadt Augsburg*, 1779:

There is also another kind of glass painting, namely one of fine beaten silver... The pictures were engraved from behind by hand.[40]

Figure 3.24 *Shepherd and Shepherdess*, South Germany (Augsburg?), 2nd half 18th century, glass size: about 13.5 x 20.5 cm (5 x 8 in.). HGS 498

Technique
Silver engraving.
Applied silver, engraved and backed with black paint.
Painted with opaque blue paint.

Figure 3.25 *Abraham and Isaak*, South Germany (Augsburg?), 2nd half 18th century, glass size: 12.8 x 20.4 cm (5 x 8 in.). HGS 329.

Technique
Gold engraving.
Applied gold, engraved and backed with black paint.
Painted with opaque blue paint.

19th century

During the course of the 19th century in central Europe, production of glass paintings reached new heights. In some areas painters became known by name but, in retrospect, the majority worked in anonymity. For small, sometimes remote communities, the availability of engravings for use as templates increased output greatly. Mass-production kept prices affordable for local customers but the inclusion of gold or *Schlag*, which is imitation gold leaf, into the picture raised the price.

Figure 3.27. *Cross*, Bohemia, 1st half 19th century, overall size: 37 x 18.5 cm (14½ x 7¼ in). HGS 495

Technique
Eglomisé
Painted black outlines (figure).
Backed with gold leaf, or probably yellow lacquer backed with silver.
Painted with black paint.

The Painter, Gilder, and Varnisher's Companion, by William T. Brannt, shows how techniques have changed little over the centuries. First published in Philadelphia in 1871, it is a veritable treasure chest of recipes for burnishing and matt gilding on glass.

Figure 3.26 *St Joseph and Child*, North Bohemia, probably Vincenz Janke, Haida (1769–1838), about 1800, overall glass size: 29 x 19.3 cm (11½ x 7½ in.). HGS 472.

Technique (centre)
Painted with opaque paint.

Technique (border)
Wheel cut glass.
Backed with gold and silver le.
Painted with red lacquer.
Backed with metal foil.

Gilding glass.

Thoroughly clean the glass, then take some very weak isinglass size, heat it, and float the glass, where the gold is to be laid, with the warm size and a soft brush. Then lay the gold on with a gilder's tip, previously drawing it over the hair of your head to cause the gold to adhere to it. Tilt the glass to allow the superfluous size to run away, then let it dry, and if it does not look sufficiently solid upon the face, give another layer of gold the same way. Where the black lines are to show, take a piece of pointed fire-wood, cut to the width the lines are needed, and with a straight-edge draw a line with the piece of wood which, if made true and smooth, will take the gold off clean, and so square and sharpen up all the edges, lines, etc. When this is done give a coat of Brunswick black thinned with a little oil of turpentine and the lines will show black, and it will preserve the gold. Try a small piece first, so as to get all in order.

Gilding glass and porcelain.

Dissolve in boiled linseed oil an equal weight either of copal or amber, and add as much oil of turpentine as will enable you to apply the compound or size thus formed, as thin as possible, to the parts of the glass intended to be gilt. The glass is to be placed in a stove till it is so warm as almost to burn the fingers when handled. At this temperature the size becomes adhesive, and a piece of leaf gold, applied in the usual way, will immediately stick. Sweep off the superfluous portions of the leaf; and when quite cold it may be burnished, taking care to interpose a piece of India paper between the gold and the burnisher.

It sometimes happens, when the varnish is not very good, that by repeated washing the gold wears off, on this account the practice of burning it in is sometimes had recourse to. For this purpose, some gold-powder is ground with borax, and in this state applied to the clean surface of the glass by a camel's-hair pencil; when quite dry, the glass is put into a stove, heated to about the temperature of an annealing oven, the gums burns off, and the borax cements the gold with great firmness to the glass; after which it may be burnished.[41]

20th century

It was perhaps inevitable that a slump would follow the high times. However, gilding on glass did not quite disappear. In 1913, Ernst Wessels met a growing interest in the subject with his publication, *Hinterglasmalerei*. He gave the following instructions:

The best adhesive or size for a burnish gilding behind glass is dissolved (clear as glass) gelatine... Place it in cold water and quickly heat. It is reckoned a half diamond of gelatine to 1 litre of water. For the best work, chemically cleaned water is necessary. Take care to use only clean receptacles and to have the cleanest working conditions in order to have a good gild. After a short time cooking let the mix cool to 60 deg. Maintain this temperature for the gilding. Then, with an absolutely clean

Figure 3.28. *St. Georgius*, probably Nikolaus Träger, Schweinfurt, 2nd half 19th century, glass size: 28 x 21.8 cm (11 x 8½ in.). HGS 140.

Technique
Painted with red, green, blue and brown lacquer, partially engraved (*églomisé*).
Painted with opaque paint.
Backed with gold leaf.

brush, which is shaken after every dip into the size, apply a thin coat of gelatine to small areas of the clean glass and gild immediately. After drying you must rub the gold with a soft silk ball and polish until it is a high burnish.

Matt gilding behind glass is much simpler. Lay small areas of *mixtion* (laying oil). When the gold size will only just hold the gold, you can gild. You have to test to find the exact time to lay the leaf. Depending on the temperature, you can test between 12 and 24 hours.[42]

21st century

Today, reverse gilding and painting on glass is enjoying a revival. Echoing the past, it is popular in interiors as wall coverings, screens, tabletops, furniture inserts and is also finding a role in jewellery design.

4

THE GILDER'S TOOLS

As well as describing the gilders' tools, this chapter also discusses the glass and metal leaf used in gilding. A number of suppliers are given on pages 70–71 and you may be able to make some of them yourself. For many of the tools there are choices. Ask the sales people about the finer points and you can decide which tool is best for you. The Glossary, page 67, will explain many of the terms. The materials are discussed in the next chapter.

A gilder on glass will need the following equipment:

* Black paper or cloth, for placing beneath gilded glass
* Brushes: squirrel mops for laying water-based size (soft and capable of holding a good amount of liquid); sable or synthetic sable for painting on glass, both round and flat; string-bound gesso brush (only if using gesso)
* Clean rag
* Cork blocks for propping up glass and to wrap sandpaper around
* Cottonwool or cotton balls for cleaning glass and burnishing leaf
* Felt tip pens for marking up the design on the front, alcohol soluble
* Gilder's tools: knife, cushion and single and double or large tips
* Heatproof container for size, such as a ceramic coffee cup
* Imitation leaf for backing or covering translucent paint and stained shellacs
* Measuring jug
* Metal flux brushes (as used for stained glass) cut down, for shading
* Palettes, plastic, glass or ceramic tiles
* Palette knives for mixing paint, including an elbow knife

* Pumice powder for distressing, cleaning glass of unwanted leaf
* Rulers
* Styluses: wooden, ivory, bone, bamboo, for engraving the gold
* Vaseline, a little for the gilder's tip
* One of the following: Wet-or-dry silicon carbide paper, 200 grit/diamond pad/Arkansas stone, wetted with water for smoothing the edges of glass
* Whiting: ground chalk, for cleaning glass mixed to a paste with alcohol or meths

Figure 4.1 Gilder's cushion, knife and tip

The cushion

Traditionally made from calfskin stretched over a padded board, approx. 23 x 15 cm (9 x 6 in.), it has a parchment shield over three sides at one end to protect from draughts. Some people make their own, but I consider a professionally made cushion well worth the investment; you will probably never need another. Some people use a pounce bag with chalk inside it to occasionally dust the cushion and to prevent a build-up of grease. Or, from time to time the surface can be kept fresh by drawing the gilding knife across the surface, left to right, to remove surface accretions, and then turning the cushion upside down and thumping the back to shake the dust away.

The gilder's knife

Available in all shapes, weights and sizes, they are quite different from one another so it is a matter of taste. French knives tend to be light (as do the Japanese bamboo knives) while English ones tend to be heavy, but the important thing is the balance; it needs to rest in the hand without tipping over. The blade can be honed on fine sandpaper to be sharp enough to cut the leaf without cutting the leather. It must be kept clean and dry: no water, grease or dirt of any kind. Hold it by the handle only.

The gilder's tip

These come in various widths and thicknesses. Most are of squirrel hair but some of the heavier ones are made with badger hair. I would suggest a full width medium tip for most uses. The heavier tips are designed for silver leaf, which used to be thicker than it is today. Silver can be very light and a regular tip will do fine. Apply a light smear of Vaseline to your left forearm (if you are right handed) and draw the hair of the tip across your arm so it picks up the lightest coat. This will help the leaf to stick to the tip. Or else draw the hairs vertically up across your brow, where there lies a residue of sweat. Draw it from the eyes upwards, pressing your free hand against the hairs of the tip. After some use the tip may get clogged up with Vaseline and bits. You can wash the hair by holding the tip so the hairs are submerged in warm soapy water. Don't let the card get wet. Rinse in the same manner with clear water a couple of times, then press between two layers of towel to soak up as much moisture as possible. Lay flat, comb the hair out and leave to dry away from direct heat.

Double tips

These are made in order to have two points of contact when laying whole leaves. One tip is laid over the other and taped together. A cork is glued on as a handle. There is also available a special tip, with handle, which is lowered on to the leaf and when lifted the leaf is attached quite firmly. (Type 'Smith tip' into a search engine and you should find details of it and a video, made in 2007, showing how to use it.) In this way it is possible to gild vertical glass.

GLASS

The quality and quantity of glass painting was always dependent on the availability of glass. As glass production technology improved, the highest quality clear rolled, cylinder or crown glass was deemed suitable for costly, commissioned work but less clear, imperfect glass was reserved for mass-produced paintings. Before float glass, molten glass was cast between two rollers and polished smooth by hand.

In the 1950s, Sir Alastair Pilkington developed a system of supporting molten glass on a bed of liquid tin which cooled with a perfectly smooth finish of uniform thickness. This is an easily available, commonly used glass; a very flat, hard and shiny surface on which to work. The reflections are clear, straight and unforgiving. The side of glass that has been in contact with the bed of tin is known as the 'tin side', the other, the 'air side'. Possibly there is a difference in reaction of paints on each side but I have found this to be of no consequence as far as gilding and painting is concerned. It is possible to detect the tin side with a special detector lamp. Placed on the tin side of the glass, it fluoresces and produces a milky white image caused by short-wave UV radiation. Placed on the non-tin side there is no reaction.

For larger sizes and for interior use, such as wall panels and tabletops, toughened glass is often used. This cannot be cut once it has been through the toughening or tempering process. It will only shatter, harmlessly, when hit sharply on a corner with a hammer. It has been through a process of heating followed by rapid cooling, during which procedure the exterior surfaces are put in rapid compression, the interior in tension: compressive forces give glass great strength. This can result in difficulties with laying leaf. No matter how clean the surface is, it can sometime repel the size and cause all sorts of problems.

Ordinary window glass tends to be green in colour. This hardly matters when painting is dark or on the cool, blue/green end of the spectrum, but white and warm pale colours could appear dirty. In these cases it may be advisable to select a glass with a reduced iron content.

Newly-blown glass is a delight to work on. Not having come into contact with anything but air, the surface is unlike any other glass surface. This is in marked contrast to recycled, old glass whose surface will be patinated with texture, though it may be hard to see with the naked eye.

Glass specialists should be consulted if in doubt about the appropriate thickness of large panels and their installation. Coloured glass is best avoided when gilding as the beauty of the precious metal will be obscured.

In short any clear, smooth glass of any thickness can be water gilded. The beauty of precious leaf behind coloured glass will be lost. If the surface is rough, it will not take water gilding, but it will take matt gilding. The cheapest glass is regular float window glass from your local glaziers; ask them to give you offcuts on which to practise.

LEAF
Gold leaf

Gold for gilding is reduced from gold bars into extremely thin leaves by a process of milling through rollers and then beating with hammers. The purity of gold is measured by dividing it into 24 parts, known as karats (kt). Pure gold, which is a little too soft to use, is 24 kts, whereas 9 kt leaf, for example, is made of only 9 parts of gold. Other metals, such as silver or copper, are added to the gold to make an alloy. These additional metals strengthen it and affect its colour. Copper will redden and warm the leaf; silver and palladium will cool it and lighten the tone. The higher the proportion of tarnishing metals, such as silver and copper, is added to the alloy the higher are the chances of the leaf oxidising. Pure gold will never tarnish.

White gold

The term 'white gold' refers to alloys of gold that appear white due to the content of precious metals such as palladium or silver.

> **Coverage**
> One book of gold or white gold will cover 1.5 square feet, so 7 books will cover 1 square metre (10–11 sq ft).

Imitation leaf

Imitation leaf, also known as Composition Leaf, Dutch Metal, Dutch Gold and *Schlag*, is made from a combination of aluminium, brass, zinc and copper. Aluminium imitates silver and alloys of the other metals imitate gold. Any of these can be used with acrylic metal leaf adhesive for backing up coloured glazes. With the exception of aluminium leaf, which will not oxidise, imitation leaf will discolour if used with oil size. None of this leaf is suitable for water gilding and I do not recommend working with it as practice for the real thing. It is generally too heavy to use with a water-based size and will just tear if engraved.

Tarnishing

Once leaf is sealed with paint and all air excluded, no discolouration should occur as long as oil size is not used. For storage, all tarnishable leaf should be kept carefully wrapped in paper and in a drawer. Some gilders keep their leaf wrapped in plastic.

Loose and transfer, or patent leaf

Loose leaf is placed between leaves of tissue, stitched together to form a book of 25 leaves. Individual leaves are separated by sheets of tissue. Transfer leaf has been attached to tissue paper with a very light wax. The leaf is released from the backing tissue when pressure is applied. It is intended for exterior surface gilding, where conditions prevent the use of loose leaf. Generally, transfer is not needed for glass decoration. For an oil-gilded surface (or one prepared with metal leaf adhesive) loose leaf is preferable as the action of pressing transfer can diminish the brightness of the gold.

Figure 4.2 Peter Binnington, design Tim Gosling.

Technique
Water gilded palladium leaf.
Distressed and backed with oil-based paints.

Figure 4.3 Bruce Jackson, kitchen splashback.

Technique
Water gilded Chinese calligraphy in 23 kt gold.
Water gilded silver leaf for the background.

Figure 4.4 *Australian Menagerie*, one of four large-scale works commissioned by Cunard for luxury cruise ship *Queen Mary 2*. Christianson Lee Studios. 168 x 457 cm (5.5 x 15 ft)

Technique
Water gilded and engraved.
Oil-based paint to cover.

❧ 5 ❧

UNDERSTANDING MATERIALS

Layers of materials on glass

In the course of gilding and painting on glass, layers of water-, oil- and shellac-based materials can be applied over one another in various combinations. Processes are carried out in reverse order from working on a canvas or a wall; hence water gilding, also known as burnish gilding, comes first on the newly cleaned glass, followed by layers of back-up or covering which might be more gilding (either burnished or matt), layers of paint, gesso, shellac or *découpage*. It is essential to understand the nature of each medium used, particularly when working on a support of smooth glass, for without the benefit of firing, which securely bonds paint to glass, decoration can delaminate or separate from the base.

This understanding will increase the chances of long-term stability. Generally it is a good plan to change materials with each process to prevent one layer disturbing its predecessor. So, applying successive thin layers of oil-based paint should present no problem, as the process is the same as painting conventionally with oil paint on a canvas or a wall, but in this case in reverse order. However, water gilding followed by painting, further followed by oil gilding are three different processes, which may or may not react to one other. Misapprehension of their behaviour can lead to disappointing accidents.

Paint (and gold) can be cleanly stripped from glass by the use of the wrong kind of shellac as a final covering. Similarly, a final layer of (protective) self-adhesive aluminium foil, necessary if a glass panel is to be glued to a wall, will also strip every layer down to the glass if any attempt is made to remove the foil. Oil-based materials, such gold size, will not disturb water-based gilding; nor will, for example, a layer of shellac disturb a layer of asphaltum, which is a tar-based pigment in oil, while on the other hand a layer of pale, oil-based paint over that same asphaltum could be a catastrophe.

Knowledge is key in order to use these processes successfully.

Materials explained

Solvents or thinners

The consistency of paint is controlled by the addition of solvents or thinners, such as water for gesso or mineral spirits for oil-based paint. The materials used for glass gilding and painting can be categorised into three groups:

1. Water-based
Solvent: water.
Materials: gelatine, gesso, metal leaf adhesive, water-based paints.

2. Oil-based
Solvents: mineral spirits, paint thinners, turpentine, turps substitute, white spirit.
Materials: sign-writers' enamels, artists' oil colours, Japan oil size, old oil size (*mixtion*), asphaltum, glaze medium, varnishes.

3. Alcohol- or meths-based
Solvents: alcohol, denatured alcohol, methylated spirits (meths), 91% isopropyl alcohol.
Material: shellac with or without stains and dyes.

Binders

The binder of paint, also known as the 'medium' or 'vehicle', carries the pigment, stain or dye.

Examples of three binders.

- ❧ For traditional gesso the binder is rabbitskin glue.
- ❧ For oil paint the binder is oil.

❀ For shellac (as used in this book), the binder is de-waxed pale polish.

(De-waxed polish will be less resistant to further coats of material, such as sign-writers paint.)

1. Water-based materials

Gelatine size
This can be made from:

❀ Isinglass: dried, shredded bladder from the sturgeon fish.
❀ Gelatine capsules as used in the medical profession.
❀ Sheet gelatine, as used for cooking.

Glue and size made from gelatine, including isinglass and sheet gelatine, is prepared by soaking in cold water and heating through. Size for glass gilding is very weak and will only hold up for about half a day, after which it cannot be relied upon to attach the leaf to the glass. A new batch then has to be made.

Gesso, traditional
This is a chalk and glue mixture used to prime panels and canvases for oil or tempera painting and to fill the grain of carved furniture and frames prior to water gilding. On glass, it was mainly used over engraved gold leaf and asphaltum to decorate glass panels used as furniture inserts, produced in the U.S.A. and the U.K. in the early 19th century.

Gesso can be coloured with dry pigments (mixed to a paste with a little water first) or with gouache or other water-based paints as a final coat. It cannot take anything wet over it as it is a porous layer. On drying, coloured gesso will be considerably lighter than when wet.

Figure 5.1 One of two overmantel panels by Peter Binnington, 93cm x 46.5cm (36.5 in x 18.5 in)

Technique
Water gilded moon gold
Engraving
Water gilded white gold
More engraving
Metal leaf adhesive, with a roller
Japanese black silver leaf

Metal leaf adhesive

This is an alternative size for oxidising leaf, such as silver, copper, Dutch metal or alloys of these metals. It can be difficult to use, especially on glass. As the work is seen from underneath, through a layer of glass, brushstrokes, normally covered, will be revealed. Stippling the size usually resolves this, but water-based size can 'go off' quite suddenly. This means it starts to set and become unworkable and will not allow manipulation. This can be resolved by the use of a roller or by applying with a soaked ball of cotton or cottonwool. Be very careful to wash any brush you are using immediately in plenty of water.

Water-based paints

In the past, water-based paints such as tempera were used to outline compositions for reverse glass paintings; the colours were later filled in with oil-based paints. Traditional tempera, made with egg, dries very hard, but acrylic water-based paints next to glass are best avoided as they have a poor hold over the long term. If they must be used, it would be better to apply a layer of oil-based material first, such as a thin clear varnish, and allow it to dry thoroughly, for at least a week if possible, before water-based paint is applied. Warning: water-based paints dry fast and might cause crazing if laid too soon over slower-drying oil-based media.

2. Oil-based materials

Sign-writers' enamel paints

Some years ago a company called Keeps manufactured a sign-writers' paint known as Intenso. It was popular and widely used in the trade and then discontinued. Happily, these paints are available again, known now as Japan colours, Intenso style. These are heavily pigmented, fast-drying paints especially formulated for decorative applications for furniture and for painting on glass. They cover well and dry quickly but their low oil content means they will remain soft. It is generally advisable to apply a further protective coat, such as a light shellac, oil- or water-based varnish or self-adhesive foil, if the work is not going to be framed. The softness of the paint will allow it to be engraved, once dry, with a wooden or steel stylus, followed by either oil gilding, with oil- or water-based size, or a further coat of paint of contrasting colour. In addition there is a range known as One Shot Enamels which are suitable for glass. They are gloss, unlike the Intenso matt range, and can be rather oily.

Some companies offer 'Reducers', which are simply thinners.

Artists' oil colours

For glass, these paints are best used to alter the colour of sign-writers' paints. With so much oil in their mix they will neither cover well nor dry if used alone. A small amount of Japan oil size can be added to speed drying, but that will thin them further.

Asphaltum, also known as bitumen

This is a tar-based pigment used not only in the etching process as an acid resist, but in the preparation of road surfacing and the waterproofing of gutters and the underside of vehicles. Stronger than regular sign-writers' back-up paints, it is applied to engraved gold leaf on glass as an isolator. This means its hardness will allow abrasion of surplus leaf while the image itself is protected, even before it has completely dried. Regular matt sign-writers' paint is too soft for this. But it is also liable over (many) years to shrink, crack and pull away from the glass, lifting the gilding. Asphaltum remains reversible, as we know from the reaction on a tar-surfaced road by the warm sun. Subsequent coats of any oil-based material will reactivate it, dissolving the solvent and it will smear; it should be followed by an alcohol or meths-based medium such as shellac, or water-based material such as gesso. With its beautiful colour it was widely used on glass in the early 19th century but evidence of shrinkage and delamination can be seen in some examples of overmantels in the American Wing of the Metropolitan Museum of Art (Study section), New York, U.S.A.

Figure 5.2 Detail of an overmantel frieze, c. 1820.

Technique
Water gilding with silver leaf.
Engraved and scratched through.
Backed up with asphaltum.

Glaze medium

This viscous, transparent medium is used to thin and extend paint. Sign-writers' paints, and/or small amounts of artists' oil paints, mixed with solvent and glaze make a thin cream. Glaze is formulated to allow a longer working time in order to create textures, such as *frottage* or stippling. Sufficient drying time must be given between layers. Depths of subtle colour and texture can be built by this method.

Japan gold size

This synthetic material is mainly composed of driers and is suitable for small areas only. It is similar to, but no substitute for, gold size as it will dry too fast and unevenly. But it can be mixed half and half with 3-hour gold size for use with synthetic leaf and, like gold size, applied as thinly as possible.

Old oil gold size

Old oil size, known as oil size or *mixtion*, was made in the past with sun-thickened linseed oil. It is applied thinly to the glass, stippled out with the tip of the brush to hide brushstrokes and left until almost dry. Gold leaf is laid on to it and brushed smooth. It is not suitable for use with tarnishing leaf

such as copper, Dutch metal, silver or white gold as oxidisation will occur. Since it can take months to harden up, though it may feel dry, nothing need follow oil gilding; if required a light coat of shellac will give protection from handling. It enhances burnish gilding with its contrasting matt appearance and is used for uneven, textured surfaces.

Varnishes

Use sign-writers' back-up varnish or a water-based varnish to protect painted glass.

3. Alcohol- or meths-based material

Shellac

A coat of light shellac can be used finally to protect work or to prevent layers from disturbing one another. Asphaltum can be prevented from reactivation with a layer of light shellac. Similarly, a layer of paint that has been thinned to a wash with thinners alone, can be secured on the glass before the next oil-based layer is applied. It is not normally required when the processes are changed, such as water gilding followed by oil-based painting. There are several occasions to use shellac:

* to stabilise thin coats, as discussed above;
* as a translucent coloured lacquer (covered with foil) over engraved gold.

Figure 5.3 Stained shellac over oil-based *frottage*, covered with aluminium foil. Seen from the front.

Shellac is obtainable in a variety of forms, such as button polish or knotting, both for sealing wood. For glass painting I would recommend a light, de-waxed, shellac that will dry almost immediately. Shellac over paint on glass needs to dry fast by solvent evaporation, to avoid softening of the underlying paint layer. A second coat will lift the first, so be sure the colour is strong enough to be applied in one pass.

Warning:

❀ thicker shellacs such as button polish take a long time to dry. As they do so they will soften and lift paint and gold! Avoid them.

❀ Stained or coloured shellac can be used as a lacquer over engraved gold, under foil, as for *amelierung*, see Chapter 4.

❀ Shellac dries too fast to brush out like paint. It must be applied swiftly and in one go, no going back. Although coloured shellac is difficult to work with, the beautiful colour possible makes it worth the effort.

Cellulose

Occasionally a further material is used that is based on cellulose thinners. Such examples might be lacquers, as used for nail varnish and for car spraying, which dry fast and evenly. 'Frigiline' is a nitrocellulose lacquer widely used to protect silver and silver leaf. As it dries so fast it is applied by spraying. A thinner, or reducer is used to reduce the viscosity of the lacquer.

The next chapter, the mirror project, carefully guides you through a project with a template and illustrated step-by-step instructions on the basic principles of making glue, laying gold and silver, engraving it and backing up with oil-based paint.

Chapter 7 reiterates many of the processes but with the addition of further techniques, illustrated and described in detail. There is a certain amount of repetition over the two chapters, designed not only to secure the information, but also to avoid that annoying search through the book to find a tip you saw somewhere and which you need while you are making your piece.

⌑ 6 ⌑

THE MIRROR PROJECT

FIGURE 1 TEMPLATE

Enlarge this template by 133%, to measure 20.3 cm square (8 in. square).

This chapter is pared down to basics so the beginner can get started. Chapter 7 has extra information such as: different techniques for gilding and backing up, more on paint glazes, shellac, foil, and so on. It also gives alternative materials (e.g. gelatine in the form of capsules rather than as sheet) and other recipes.

Equipment needed for the mirror project

You will need the following (suppliers are listed in Appendix 2):

* One book each of loose (not transfer) 22 kt gold and silver leaf
* Alcohol or meths
* Apron
* Brushes: for water-based size, a squirrel mop, size 6 or 8 is ideal, but you can substitute it with a cheaper synthetic brush. For oil-based paint, one stroke flat synthetic brush, 1.9 cm (¾ in.), or a size 8.
* Clean rag
* Cork block
* Cotton or cottonwool
* Double tip or tip with handle for laying whole leaves
* Elbow palette knife
* Felt-tip permanent marker pen (waterproof)
* Gelatine (sheet, with perforations in diamonds)
* Gilder's knife, cushion and tip
* Glass cleaner
* Glass palette
* Glass, 20.3 cm square (8 in square) recycled or new window glass
* Household oil-based paint, (not gloss) or sign-writers' paint. Black or any dark colour.
* One pint heatproof measuring jug
* Paint thinners: mineral spirits/turps
* Paper towel
* Pumice powder
* Ruler: 30 cm (12 in.), plastic with guidelines
* Vaseline for lightly greasing the gilder's tip
* Whiting, which is ground chalk
* Wooden stylus and stiff brush for shading

Glass

Any clear smooth glass of any thickness can be used for water gilding. The cheapest is regular float window glass from your local glaziers; ask them to give you offcuts on which to practise.

Gilder's tools

The cushion
Traditionally made from calfskin stretched over a padded board, about 23 x 15 cm (9 x 6 in.). It has a parchment shield over three sides at one end to protect from draughts.

The gilder's knife
Available in all shapes and sizes. The important thing is the balance; it needs to rest comfortably in the hand without tipping over.

The gilder's tip
I suggest a full-width medium tip for most uses. For laying whole leaves, either make a double one as I have suggested or type 'Smith tip' into a search engine and you should find details of a specially made tip, with a video showing how to use it and obtain it.

Processes for making the mirror

1. Photocopy the template

Enlarge the template on page 34 by 133% to measure 20.3 x 20.3 cm (8 x 8 in).

2. Smooth the glass

Figure 6.2 Sanding the glass edges.

If the glass has sharp edges, take a sheet of 220 wet-or-dry silicon carbide paper, fold it in three and tear off one third. Wrap it around a cork or wooden block, dip it into cold water and rub it along the edge of the glass at an angle of 45 degrees. Do this on both sides, being careful not to scratch the glass. Include the corners.

3. Soak the gelatine

Place one diamond of sheet gelatine into the heatproof measuring jug and pour 50 ml (¼ cup) cold tapwater over it. Leave it to soak, completely submerged, while you continue (roughly 10 minutes).

4. Prepare the glass

Clean both sides of the glass. Do this in two stages:

Start with a proprietary glass cleaner that comes in a spray bottle. Spray the glass and with a clean cloth clean the glass.

Sprinkle half a teaspoon of whiting onto the glass. Moisten it with 1 tsp alcohol or meths and rub the mix evenly over the front and back with a pad of cotton or cottonwool. If it is too dry add more liquid. Let the mixture dry. The whiting will dry much lighter. When it is dry, clean off the powder completely with a dry, lint free cloth.

Figure 6.3 Whiting and alcohol mixture.

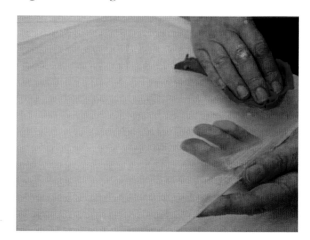

Figure 6.4 Removing the whiting.

Figure 6.5 Template and glass.

5. Mark up the glass

Remove all traces of whiting from your working area.

Place the glass over the template and position it exactly.

You are now looking at the front of the glass. All the marking out is carried out with a permanent marker on this side, and all the gilding and painting will be done on the back.

Mark the side facing you with a large F to avoid confusion. When the template and glass are lined up exactly lay your ruler along the outer edge of the meander pattern and draw a line along it from edge to edge of the glass.

Repeat on the remaining sides, which will make a border or box 1.4 cm (½ in.) from the outer edge of the glass, with a little box on each outside corner.

Now lay the ruler along the inner edge of the meander pattern and draw a box. Mark the extensions at each end. This inside box will be 7 cm (2in.) from the edge of the glass.

The centre will have one sheet of silver leaf and the meander pattern border will be gilded. Put the template aside.

6. Make the size

The gelatine needs to have soaked for a minimum of 10 minutes. It will swell in the water but will not dissolve until it is heated through.

Add 250 ml (1 cup) of very hot water to the soaking gelatine. As you add, stir well with a clean soft brush to ensure even distribution of the dissolved mixture. Top up with warm water to 500 ml (2 cups). This seems like an excessive quantity of water but do not worry. The size will keep for about half a day after which its effectiveness as glue is unreliable. Make a new batch if necessary.

Now turn the glass over.

Figure 6.6 Getting ready to lay silver leaf. Note the F is turned around.

7. Wet the glass with size

You are now going to wet the central area for the silver.

You need to break the surface tension by brushing hard until the size flows in a continuous pool. It is not possible to wet the glass too much, but confine the size to within the area to be gilded.

Figure 6.7 Laying the size. This from another example.

8. Lay the silver leaf

Open the book flat, exposing one sheet of silver leaf.

Lightly brush the tip with a small amount of vaseline (grease your arm with it first).

Hold the tip with your thumb uppermost. Do not turn it over at any stage. Lay the tip, vaselined side down, halfway along the sheet and press it down onto the leaf. Silver can be quite heavy, so the tip may need more vaseline than the gold will need. You may even need to press the edge of your hand down on the tip.

Have the glass propped on the cork block.

Once the leaf is securely on the tip, transfer the tip to your left hand (if right handed) and with your right hand wet the glass again. This is very important as the leaf will not stick on to dry glass.

Immediately put the brush down, transfer the tip to the right hand with the silver side facing the glass,

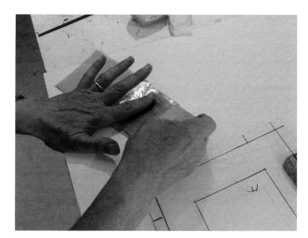

Figure 6.8 Pressing down on to the leaf.

keep your thumb on top and lay the silver onto the wet glass. You have time, so don't panic. If the leaf folds under itself just carry on. If it has not, but is merely crumpled, that is fine.

You can wet the leaf some more by taking the loaded brush to the top edge and without squeezing the excess size out on the side of the jug, letting the size run down under the leaf. With the surface completely wet under the leaf you can adjust it very carefully with a finger so it sits squarely in the centre. It may look crumpled but as it dries it will pull smooth against the glass. If there are large air bubbles you can blow them to the edge where they will pop.

Figure 6.9 Bringing the leaf towards the glass.

Figure 6.10 Placing the leaf on to the wetted glass.

Figure 6.11 Adjusting the leaf with a finger.

9. Get ready to lay gold

During this time be sure not to touch the blade of the knife or get it wet.

A light but firm touch is needed for handling gold. Roll the book gently from the spine into a cylinder, first one way then the other. This will loosen the gold from its tissue-paper backing.

Open a page of the book flat on the table.

Place the knife parallel to the open side of the book.

Tap it lightly on the table so the leaf just lifts at the edge.

Quickly slide the knife under the leaf.

Lift carefully and drop on to the cushion.

Another way of handling gold leaf:

Open the book over the opened cushion and gently blow out one leaf at a time into the back of it.

Figure 6.12 Blowing out gold on to the cushion.

Once you have three or four leaves released, put the book aside well away from moisture, slide the knife under one leaf and gently bring it to the front of the cushion. Try to lay it square. When it is in position, but crumpled, aim a sharp but *gentle* breath to the centre, which will spread the leaf out flat. It's a tricky technique, but courage and practice will pay off.

Practise picking it up and laying it down flat again. If you tear it, don't worry but try again with a new piece. Gold sticks to itself, you will find. If the leaf folds over on itself it may be possible to open it up and save it, but it is likely some leaf will be ruined. Keep gold fragments in the back of the cushion; they will be useful later.

10. Gild the border

You will be gilding just over the lines you have drawn, but not to the edge of the glass, keeping the extensions clear.

Wet the area along the whole left side of the silver, top to bottom. Be generous, but don't splash the size about and try not to get it on the silver.

Bring a leaf of gold to the front of the cushion and once it is flat cut it in half, laying the knife along it, pressing down firmly, pushing forward and back.

Figure 6.13 Cutting the leaf.

Pick up one piece by firmly laying the tip onto it, but no hand pressure this time, and when it is securely on, transfer hands and wet the glass again.

As quickly as you can repeat what you did with the silver: put the brush down, switch hands again and lay the leaf in the top left-hand corner. It is most important the glass is sufficiently wetted before you lay. If the silver is drying try not to let size run over it. If you need to, turn the glass as you go round so this will not happen.

Let the gold jump on to the size in one firm action. Don't let it grab the water at one end, rather all the gold has to hit the size at once with a positive, slapping action. Bring the tip away sharply when you judge the two, gold and size, have made contact.

Figure 6.14 Wetting for the first leaf of gold.

Lay from top to bottom, letting each leaf hang on to its neighbour. Once the left side is done, lay across the top, then down the right-hand side, and finally across the bottom. Cut smaller pieces to patch, always wetting first with a smaller brush, and then stand the glass up to dry. Try not to get size on top of the gold.

Figure 6.15 Laying first gold leaf in top left-hand corner.

Figure 6.16 Preparing to lay leaf across the top.

Figure 6.17 Wetting before laying down the right-hand side.

Figure 6.18 Finishing the right-hand side.

Figure 6.19 Cutting smaller sections for patching.

Figure 6.20 Patching.

Figure 6.21 Completed gilding.

11. Stand up to dry

Lean the glass against something solid so the size can run off quickly. A good circulation of air is best for drying. If you can stand it near a draft and see the loose leaf blowing in the breeze the leaf will dry well, even if the temperature is not high. Use a hair drier, gently, if you are in a hurry. As the leaf dries it pulls flat over the glass and many creases come out naturally. If you are not sure if it is dry, look at the front. If there are wet patches they will show dull against the dry, shiny gold.

Figure 6.22 Standing it vertical to dry.

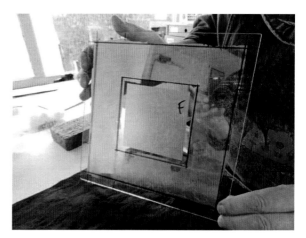

Figure 6.23 Leaf partially dry, seen from the front.

12. Burnish and patch

Let the leaf dry completely before continuing.

Burnishing smoothes out the gold leaf and gives it a polish. Burnish with cotton or cottonwool, very gently at first. Be sure the gold is securely attached to the glass and quite dry before you burnish harder to achieve a mirror-like reflection.

Figure 6.24 Catching the skewings.

If a lot of gold comes away, and this is the most common problem with beginners, it will be because there was not enough size on the glass. Collect the skewings in a jam jar (the bits you brush off).

Patch the bald areas by cutting the leaf into smaller pieces, always straight so you are not left with odd shaped scraps.

Wet the glass with a smaller brush and pop in the patches. If a lot has come away cut larger patches and use the tip. It is easier to pick up very small patches with a little, soft paintbrush. Check first you are patching within the border. You can always patch after the first light engraving into the gold to be sure of patching only where necessary.

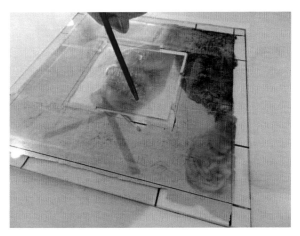

Figure 6.25 A small patch is needed.

13. Engrave

Engraving is a process whereby the gold is removed from the glass with sharpened instruments such as a wooden stick, ivory or bamboo. The surface of the glass remains intact. The marks made will show up when the gold is covered with paint and the finished work turned around.

With a ruler and a wooden stylus scribe the main lines along the outer edge and using the extension marks, locate the inner box and scribe that without scratching through the gold border.

Place the glass over the template so the two line up precisely.

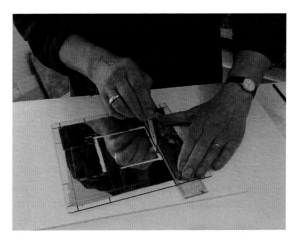

Figure 6.26 Scribing lines following the guidelines drawn on the front of the glass.

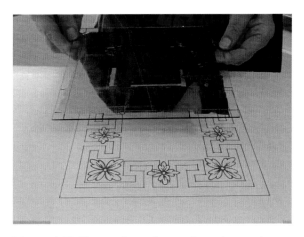

Figure 6.27 Glass and template are brought together.

If you cannot see the design through the gold, take some pumice on a finger and very gently rub the gold until you can.

Using the wooden stylus, lightly trace through the main lines of the design. Be careful when drawing not to touch the leaf too much with your hand. Grease from your skin can make it hard to engrave; a piece of paper over the gold will protect the gilding as you work. At this point you are only lightly sketching in the design. Later you will have the chance to draw it out properly. Once you have indicated the main lines, remove the template and replace it with black paper or cloth.

Figure 6.28 Rubbing through to see the design beneath.

Figure 6.29 The design is drawn out enough to carry on without the template.

Figure 6.30 The pattern roughed out and the waste gold around the edges removed.

Use the plastic ruler with its lines to help you draw out the meander pattern.

Once the pattern is drawn out and all the waste gold removed, with the help of the ruler trim the edges of the silver leaf so they are square, or you can leave it whole, just as it came in the book.

Figure 6.31 Trimming the silver square with the ruler.

To remove scraps of gold and silver around the pattern rub them away with a little pumice on a finger most carefully. This is a good way to age the gold and silver, to soften their sharp edges.

Figure 6.32 Tidying up and aging the gilding.

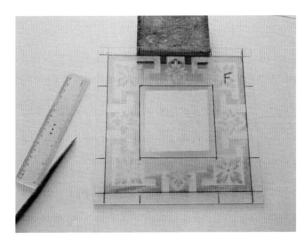

Figure 6.33 The finished engraving, the guidelines still in place, seen from the front.

Once the engraving is all done and the waste removed, turn the glass over, place it on a cloth and hold it firm while you remove the permanent marker from the front. Do not let the glass move or the gilding may scratch. You can use extra-fine steel wool for this or a rag with a little alcohol or meths.

Figure 6.34 Cleaning the front with very fine steel wool.

14. Cover with oil-based paint

With your palette knife take some black or dark-coloured paint from the tin and put it onto the glass palette.

Dip a flat brush into solvent, mineral spirits or white spirit, mop the excess on to a paper towel and mix the paint to make it workable.

Figure 6.35 Mixing up the paint on a glass palette.

Paint across the whole back. There is nothing to stop you painting different colours, as long as the paint is oil-based. Dark paint shows the gold up well.

Figure 6.36 The first coat of black paint.

The paint may not appear to cover well, and if you hold the glass up to the light and view the front you will not be happy with the coverage. But this glass will be seen by reflected, not transmitted light. View the front with the light blocked, against the black cloth; it will look better. You can apply a second coat once this one is dry.

Figure 6.38 The same glass held with no light allowed through.

Figure 6.37 Light coming through the first layer of paint. Seen from the front.

15. The finished mirror

Two coats of paint should be sufficient covering if the glass is to be framed. See Chapter 7 for advice on washing your brushes and Chapter 8 for safety hazards you should be aware of.

Figure 6.39 The finished mirror ready to be framed and hung on the wall.

7

FURTHER PROCESSES
AND RECIPES

This chapter recapitulates some of the information given in earlier chapters and adds to the techniques described in Chapter 6. It is worth remembering that cold gilding and painting on glass is distinguished from other types of glass painting by the following:

* Processes are carried out on the underside of the glass.
* The first process is always water (burnish) gilding while the glass is super clean, followed by oil-based back-up colours/shellac/matt gilding/collage or a combination of all.
* The finished panel is turned around finally so lettering must be drawn backwards and all imagery will be reversed, just like in printmaking.

Gilding, whether on glass, metal, wood or any base, is either burnished (shiny) or matt (dull). Burnish gilding on glass reflects like a mirror and tends to be dark. Any kind of contamination, such as a deposit of chalk after cleaning or smears of solvent will prevent a good gild: a good burnish could be difficult and engraving a problem.

Matt gilding scatters the light and appears lighter in tone than burnish gilding. It can be carried out at a later stage, after all the water gilding and engraving has been completed. Since it has a rubbery base, it is not suitable for engraving.

The following topics are reiterated in this chapter:

* Cleaning and marking up of glass.
* Water gilding: burnishing, laying whole leaf, covering large areas, steaming and double gilding, distressing, skewings, water gilding with skewings.
* Matt gilding – water-based metal leaf adhesive, oil-based 3-hour gold size.
* Painting glazes.
* Coloured shellac stains for backing with foil.
* How to transfer a design – transposing a mirror image design, engraving, engraving through sign-writers paint.
* Backing up – asphaltum, gesso, *découpage*, shellac.
* Cleaning up – washing brushes.

Cleaning

Be sure to remove all traces of chalk from the cleaning process before gilding. On a large panel this can take longer than it might appear. It is worth taking the trouble as the smallest trace of chalk will contaminate your gild. (See chapter 6, section 4, page 36 for more information on this topic.)

Marking up of the glass

You can spend as long as you like drawing your design directly on to the front of the glass. Use a permanent marker, easily removable with alcohol or meths on a cloth. Before you start be clear which areas are to be gilded; if you have a design on paper already (and you are happy it will be reversed) place it beneath the glass and trace the outside edge of the area to be gilded. There is no need to trace every feather and leaf; you are only indicating where the gold is to be laid. (See chapter 6, section 5, page 37.)

Figure 7.1 Marking out the glass.

Gelatine size

This can be made from sheet perforated gelatine, 1 diamond to 1 pint or 500 ml water, or from capsules, size 00, using one half capsule (either half) to the same quantity of water. Gelatine size, the thin, water-based glue used for water gilding, is very weak and good for only half a day or so before it begins to break down and lose its adhesive properties, so always mix it fresh. (See chapter 6, section 3, page 36.)

Water/burnish gilding

If you feel the need to practise before going on to gold leaf, use silver leaf rather than Dutch metal or *Schlag*. That, like aluminium leaf, is too heavy to water gild. That category of leaf will not hang onto the glass and will tear if you try to engrave it, but silver, though not as thin as gold, can be water gilded, burnished and engraved, just like gold. (See chapter 6, section 8, page 38.)

Laying whole leaf, silver and gold

There are several methods for laying whole leaves. The picture of Bruce Jackson in Chapter 1 (page 1) shows him using a single, thick tip to lay silver. Many years ago I was taught to make and use a double tip.

- You need: two single tips; white, wood glue.
- Overlap one over the other so the total area of hair is extended to about 9 cm (3½ in).
- Glue the card surfaces together with a little glue.
- Take a cork from a wine or champagne bottle and glue that onto the back of the tip, for a handle.
- Leave the glue to set.
- Lightly grease the hairs of the tip with vaseline and hold it by its handle in your left hand (if you are right handed).
- Press down on to the leaf, or else slide the knife all the way under it, 2.5 cm (1 in.), from the outer edge and flip it over onto the tip.

Figure 7.2 Lifting silver leaf from the book on to a double tip.

Lift the loaded knife up and bring it towards you flipping the leaf over squarely onto the tip. The silver may not sit firmly on the tip, or may want to fly away. Blow it firmly and squarely onto the lightly greased hair and with luck it will stay there.

Figure 7.3 Flipping the silver leaf onto the double tip.

Put the knife down somewhere clean and dry. Keeping the tip in the left hand, wet the glass with your right. Put the brush away.

Figure 7.4 The leaf firmly secured on the tip, in left hand.

Transfer the loaded tip to the right hand, swiftly bring it down over the wetted glass and let the leaf make contact all at once with the size.

Figure 7.5 Bringing the leaf down with the right hand.

If the leaf is down and you want to re-position it, but there is a dry spot preventing this, try running size down under the leaf, from a loaded brush. This should loosen the leaf and allow movement. This works with silver, as it is heavy, but gold is a bit too delicate to reposition and I would suggest you do not touch that once it is laid, even though it is tempting. *Do not* try to lay leaf, either gold or silver, unless it is attached sufficiently to the tip. You need total control over it and if it is only just hanging on you will not be able to lay it accurately.

As you can see, there are several ways of handling leaf and with practice you will find the best for you.

Covering large areas

Laying whole leaf on large panels is often best with the glass vertical, on an easel or propped against a steady support. Work from top to bottom, left to right – as if painting a wall. This way you have only one wet edge. If you need to have a break and leave the work, wipe away any dried size with a clean soft cloth when you are ready to resume. The panel may be too large to handle with one span, so it can be divided into sections. In Chapter 1, you can see Bruce Jackson has placed a gridded paper guide behind the glass. The grid can also be drawn directly on to the front of the glass and removed later.

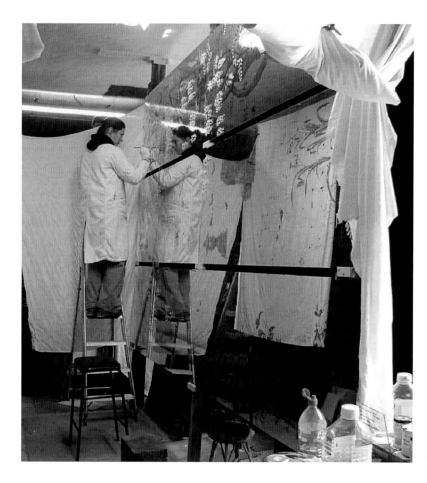

Figure 7.6 Working large scale, courtesy Peter Binnington.

Steaming and double gilding

After burnishing, the gold can be made shinier by steaming the glass. Let the steam from a boiling kettle pass between the gold and the glass. The gold will change in appearance when the steam makes contact. Do not leave the steam playing on the gold, but pass it across in one smooth action. If the gold lifts in blisters don't panic, just leave it to pull flat again by itself. The steam is reactivating the gelatine so the least amount is left on the glass, leaving the gold shinier.

> **Double gilding (second layer of gilding)**
>
> Burnish the first layer of laid leaf.
>
> Make new size and apply evenly all over the area.
>
> Gild.

It is not easy to do this, as the size will want to bead up. Use tepid rather than very warm size. Keep wetting as necessary.

Distressing for an antique effect

Pumice powder will distress the gold to achieve an antique effect. This can be rubbed gently over the glass with the fingers or with an old piece of felt. For silver leaf that is to be distressed it is easier to control if you use a stronger size, such as 2 diamonds (or capsules) to 500 ml (2 cups) water.

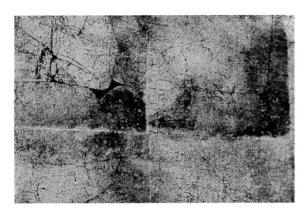

Figure 7.7 Distressed silver leaf backed with dark paint.

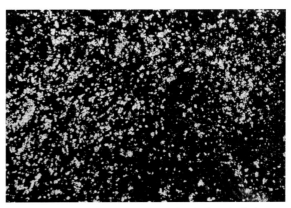

Figure 7.8 Water gilded skewings backed with dark paint.

Effects with skewings

After the gild has dried you can brush the surface with a very soft mop, brushing any overlapping pieces of gold into a folded piece of paper and from there into a jam jar. Use for effects such as the Milky Way, plankton, gold dust, etc. Each of these can be represented by the use of tiny, powdery particles of gold or silver on a dark field.

> **Water gilding with skewings**
>
> Place the glass on a flat surface, or better on the floor.
>
> Wet the glass with size.
>
> Tip a quantity of skewings into a sieve and push through with a dry hog's hair paintbrush. Allow them to float down onto the size.
>
> Burnish when dry, collecting loose skewings.
>
> Experiment with distance from the glass, size of sieve, different leaf and with backing colours.
>
> Repeat to build up layers.

Painting glazes

Paint can be applied thinly as a translucent veil to be followed with further materials.

A blue-brown mix is used for this example. If your chosen colours are hard to obtain in sign-writers' paints use any oil-based paints. However, if using artists' colours use very little as they will take forever to dry. A little of each colour is laid on the glass palette and mixed with thinners to make a light cream. If you are familiar with painting techniques a certain amount of glaze medium can be added to extend the mix and strengthen it.

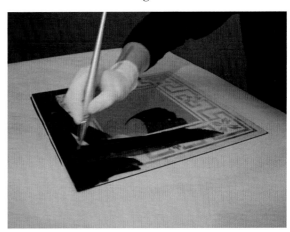

Figure 7.9 Laying on a thin coat of paint.

Frottage

To create the texture known as *frottage*, tamp the wet paint with newspaper followed by crumpled (thin) plastic. A scrunched up thin plastic bag from the supermarket will work well for this. Keep turning it as you go. Let it dry.

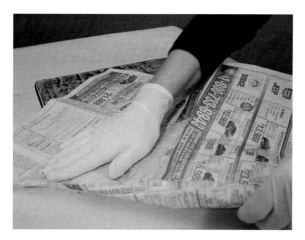

Figure 7.10 Pressing newspaper down.

Figure 7.11 Most paint removed with flat newspaper.

Figure 7.12 Removing more of the paint with a crumpled sheet of plastic, such as a thin shopping bag.

Figure 7.13 The finished *frottage*.

Coloured shellac stain for backing with foil

The purpose of this process is to provide a rich, translucent layer of colour. When it is backed with foil the reflected light actually resembles the transmitted light of stained glass. This polish or lacquer is difficult to apply evenly with a brush, due to the rapid evaporation of its alcohol-based solvent, but if you have a previous textured layer of *frottage* (see above) it helps to trick the eye and disguise any overlaps.

The lacquer is made by adding shellac to a small amount of concentrated colour. The proportion depends on the strength of colour you want. Universal tint can be used for this; a concentration available in many colours and compatible with water, oil and alcohol-based media. See Chapter 5 for more information.

You can make your own stain by obtaining a stain or dye in powder form that is soluble in alcohol or meths. To a small quantity on a glass palette add a few drops of alcohol or meths and with an elbow palette knife grind the pigment so it no longer feels gritty. Add more liquid if you need to. Mix the sticky mess with shellac until the colour is right.

Lay your polish on swiftly, moving from left to right in one sweep, with a large, well-loaded but not dripping squirrel mop. Do *not* go back on yourself as the solvent evaporates extremely fast. You will need to wait about an hour for it all to dry thoroughly before moving to the next stage.

Figure 7.14 Laying on the alcohol-based polish in even strokes.

Red polish

Figure 7.15 Completed glass ready for painting areas that are not to be backed with foil.

In this exercise foil is going to be laid over some areas only. If you were to take a piece of aluminium foil and hold it in place behind the *dry* red lacquer, then turn the glass over, you would see the effect from the front. The aim is to illuminate the red stain.

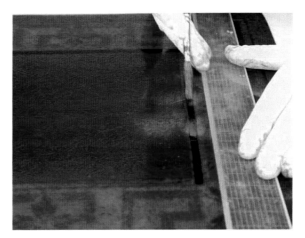

Figure 7.16 The first striping lines.

The areas *not* to have foil will need to be blocked or isolated first by a layer of opaque, oil-based paint. The purpose is to block the light and to prevent leaf showing through. Painting lines is called 'striping' and this is done with a striping brush. Paint the areas to be blocked out with a dark colour, then fill in between with a larger brush.

Use full strength sign-writers' paint mixed with only enough solvent to make it flow nicely from the brush so it covers well in one pass.

Figure 7.17 Masking areas that take no leaf.

Matt gilding

Matt gilding will be used here to attach foil to the shellac layer. It is also used if the surface is textured and too rough for water gilding. Matt works well against burnish gilding – a contrast enhanced by a change in the colour of leaf. If using matt gilding next to glass rather than over a layer of colour, be careful to stipple out the size as brushmarks will be visible once the glass is turned around.

Matt gilding is one of many techniques fully exploited by some contemporary sign-writers on glass for a variety of decorative effects. The size can be oil- or water-based, but whichever size is used, the sticky base will not allow engraving. Remember to apply either one as thinly as possible.

Applying gold size to red polish

Apply a very thin layer of 3-hour oil-based size or water-based metal leaf adhesive. For the oil size, use a flat synthetic one-stroke brush. If using water-based size, use a similar brush but wash it out immediately in warm water and keep it for water-based materials alone. Leave the size until just tacky.

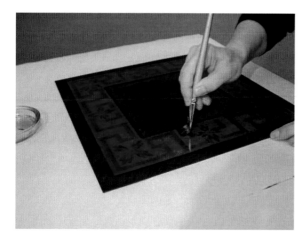

Figure 7.18 Laying a thin coat of oil size.

Cover with foil

Aluminium, copper and Dutch metal foil, like precious leaf (gold and silver), is prepared for sale interleaved with tissue paper. Much heavier than precious leaf, these foils can be handled with clean, dry hands. Cut the foil to size with scissors, (large enough to span the leaf ideally) *with* the tissue, and keep the tissue in place until the foil is secured on the glass. It is not attached to the foil and will come away easily when you want to remove but it is useful, while handling the foil, to prevent damage. A sharp blade against a straight edge will also work for cutting it.

Smooth with a soft brush and brush away the skewings. They are not worth keeping. In the illustrations I am using aluminium for the cool colour, but any of the above foils can be used for this purpose.

Figure 7.19 Laying aluminium foil.

Figure 7.20 Smoothing the leaf with a soft brush.

Figure 7.21 From the front, gold backed with *frottage*, red shellac polish, paint and foil.

How to transfer a design

If you have a design of the same size as the gilded glass you will need to transfer it. Traditional methods of pouncing rouge powder through a cartoon with holes will probably not work as you are working on a surface that is polished and hard. For the same reason it can be difficult to work with carbon paper. By following the process outlined below the design will be reversed when you turn the glass over finally. If you do not want it to be reversed (mirror image), you can remake the design by tracing it on to tracing paper, which is then turned over, then follow the process.

Transferring a design for gold or silver leaf

If the design is in mirror image (and already gilded):
Place the design under the glass, gilded side up.
Align it to be sure it is in the right position, then gently rub the leaf with your fingers and some pumice.
Once you can see the design through the abraded gold, stop rubbing and draw out the principal lines with a wooden stylus.

If you do not want to reverse the design follow this process:
Place the design under the clean glass and trace the outlines on to it.
Remove the drawing. Turn the glass over and trace your lines onto the facing side. This is now the front.
Turn it over again, to what is now the back, clean the glass thoroughly and gild.
The mapping of the design will now correspond to your drawing.

Figure 7.22. A panel partially gilded with the engraving marked out and ready to draw in freehand, over black.

Engraving

As soon as the gild is dry and has been burnished, work can start. Once the design is marked out, the paper design can be removed and replaced with black paper. Continue your engraving and it will start to feel the same as making marks with pencil on paper. This is where you can work freehand to let the imagery be as fresh as possible.

The process is much like scraperboard. It is a reductive technique – everything that you scratch away will be shown in a colour (black if you are mak-

ing the mirror project in the previous chapter). A variety of tools will remove the leaf: the simplest is a sharpened length of dowel, but ivory, bone, bamboo, metal, toothpicks, knitting needles and pencils all work. Pumice on a finger should remove remnants of unwanted leaf. If the gold or silver is to be backed with black, the *smallest* amount of residual leaf will show up, without mercy, so take care. You may want shading and texture, in which case a cutdown metal flux brush works well. Work as you would when drawing on paper, but remember the image will be reversed, as in printmaking. This only really matters in the case of lettering.

Be careful when drawing not to touch the leaf too much with your hand. Grease from your skin can make it hard to engrave; a piece of paper over the gold will protect the gilding as you work. Gelatine hardens as it ages; it is easier to engrave sometimes when the size is freshly laid.

Engraving through sign-writers' paint

As this particular paint is very soft, it can be engraved and then backed with another layer of paint. It can also be backed with foil, a method of glass gilding that goes back to the 18th century:

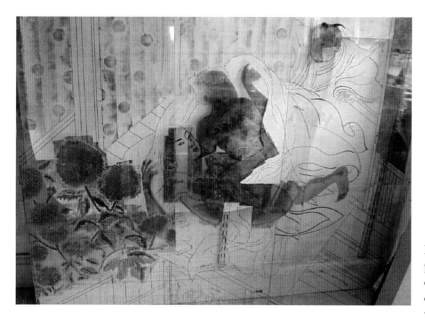

Figure 7.23 A screen in three parts, in progress. Partially gilded and painted with guidelines on the front of the glass still visible.

Figure 7.24 *Death Dance* (detail). See Chapter 3 page 18 for the whole picture.

see Chapter 4 for descriptions of early techniques. You can use either oil-based size or metal leaf adhesive to attach the foil, but water gilding will not work as there is hardly, if any, glass on to which to attach the leaf.

See Chapter 5 for a full explanation of all the materials involved.

Backing up

'Backing up' means covering the engraved leaf with a material that will protect it and provide a background colour. That could be opaque paint, a build up of glazes, which will block the light, or further layers of leaf, sometimes followed by paint or shellac.

Figures 7.25, 7.26 Front and back of gilded and painted panel, detail.

Figure 7.27 Panel from an overmantel, c. 1820: gold backed with asphaltum.

Asphaltum

Figure 7.28 Detail, showing some delamination.

In this example, the gilding was engraved and the garland painted with asphaltum. The mark of the loaded soft, pointed brush can clearly be seen in the foliage where the paint went beyond the engraved line. Once the excess gold was removed, the entire background within the border was painted black and the outer border painted with coloured gesso.

How to use asphaltum with gesso backing

See the recipe for gesso on page 61. Gild and engrave.

Back up with asphaltum, thinned to a brushing consistency with solvents, covering the areas of gilding to be preserved.

Clear away surplus leaf with pumice and saliva, with finger or with cotton or cottonwool. Saliva is very useful; it has enzymes that will break down leaf without wetting the surface too much.

Cover areas of clear glass with coloured gesso, which completes the job.

How to use asphaltum to isolate (keep separate) the gilded layer

This is necessary if followed by further layers of oil-based material. This procedure will prevent the solvent in the last oil-based layers dissolving the asphaltum.

Gild, back up with asphaltum and remove surplus leaf, as above.

Apply a layer of pale shellac polish overall, either sprayed or with a soft brush.

Leave at least one hour to dry.

Paint with oil-based paints.

How to use asphaltum as a colourless mask or isolator only

Gild, back up with asphaltum and remove surplus leaf, as above.

With a brush, wet the asphaltum with thinners and leave for some moments to loosen the paint. Do not rub.

Once loose gently press paper towel onto the glass and mop up the slurry. Repeat with clean thinners till the asphaltum is gone.

Back up with oil-based colours.

Découpage

Découpage is a term for painted or printed paper which is glued to the glass. It can be combined with a partially gilded and engraved surface, or used alone. If using items from newspapers, photocopy them first to minimise yellowing. If combining *découpage* with gilding and painting complete all water gilding first.

Figure 7.29 *Schlafende Venus mit Cupido*, Hans Jakob Sprüngli, Zürich, 1600. 29.3 x 24 cm (11½ x 9 in.)

Technique
Engraved water gilding.
Translucent laquer.
Faux hinterglasmalerei (behind-glass painting).
Tin foil.

Figure 7.30 Frances Federer, *Exodus*, 39 x 47 cm (15½ x 18½ in.).

Technique
Engraved gold leaf.
Découpage with newsprint.
Border of water-gilded gold and tarnished silver leaf.
Backed with oil-based paints.

Découpage on glass

Soak the paper cut-outs in cold water until they curl up.

Remove surplus moisture and coat front and back with watered-down white wood glue, also known as polyvinyl acetate (PVA).

Press the cutting down on to the glass.

Smooth out all air bubbles and wipe off excess. The glue becomes transparent on drying.

Once dry, a coat of light shellac will prevent backing paint from soaking through.

Gesso

Gesso is a water-based mix of whiting (calcium carbonate) and animal glue, used in the preparation of gilded furniture and frames. It is most effective on glass when applied over asphaltum, which will smear if followed by an oil-based material. Gesso covers and adheres to glass very well, unlike acrylic-based synthetic gesso, which neither covers nor adheres well.

For traditional gesso you will need

- Rabbitskin glue granules
- Whiting
- Saucepan or double boiler
- Half pint heatproof container for the gesso, to stand in the saucepan
- Hotplate
- A hog's-hair brush bound with string to mix gesso with
- Sieves
- Plastic or glass bowl
- Water-based paint
- Flat one-stroke brush with synthetic (or real) hair for applying gesso

How to make gesso

1:15 by volume of dry rabbitskin glue: water.

Soak the dry glue in cold water for a minimum of 2–3 hours or overnight.

Heat gently in a saucepan until melted. Do not boil.

Slowly add sifted gilder's whiting until it is peaking just over the size (the powder will form a pyramid that gradually dissolves into the liquid).

Leave to stand in a warm room overnight, or for a few hours while it absorbs the glue.

Wet the hog's-hair brush and shake free of excess moisture. This will reduce the chance of introducing air into the gesso.

Liquefy the glue by slowly warming it, gently stirring the mix to integrate all the whiting without introducing air bubbles.

Sieve several times through a wire mesh to blend completely. The gesso should resemble thin cream.

Store in the refrigerator and when set, cover with cold water to keep fresh.

To use: cut out pieces of the gesso to around 200 ml (¾ cup). Heat through, slowly, in a double boiler. Too much heat will cause pinholes: trapped air in tiny pockets.

To colour the gesso, add water-based paint, such as gouache or dry pigment (previously mixed into a paste with a little water). It will dry considerably lighter in tone.

Figure 7.32 detail.

Final sealing and protection

If the back needs an extra layer of protection use one light coat of sprayed or brushed-on pale shellac for framed glass panels, or sign-writers' back-up varnish. For installation work to be glued to the wall, apply self-adhesive aluminium foil across the whole back over a coat of varnish. This prevents mastic glue coming through the paint.

Figure 7.31 Silvered Regency panel from an overmantel backed with oil-based paint, asphaltum and coloured gesso.

Cleaning up

Washing brushes used in water-based materials

Use warm, soapy water. Rinse well. Shape soft hairs while wet and leave them to dry either hanging down or lying flat, standing neither on their tips nor standing upright. Keep brushes for water-based materials separate from those used for alcohol or oil-based materials.

Washing brushes used in thinners-based paints

Wipe surplus paint from brushes on a cloth. Dip into a solvent such as mineral spirits, turpentine or white spirit and wipe again. Repeat a few times. When most of the paint is removed, immerse the brush in hot, soapy water. It can be left to stand. You will see the reaction of the oil and water as the two solvents repel each other. Leave to stand for a few minutes or up to half an hour. The soapy water can be changed and at any point the brush is washed by thoroughly mixing soap into the bristles in the palm of the hand. You can be very firm with the brush, bending the brush hard at the ferrule end to check that all colour has been removed. Repeat until clean. Rinse and leave brushes lying flat to dry.

Washing brushes used in alcohol-based shellac

Rinse well in alcohol or meths. and then in warm soapy water until all colour is gone. Leave hanging upside down or lying flat to dry.

Videos

There are several helpful videos of processes described in this and the previous chapter on the internet that can be found with keyword searches, such as 'gilding glass', *verre églomisé*, 'gold leaf', 'Smith tip'.

8

PROBLEM SOLVING AND SAFETY ADVICE

A host of problems can arise when gilding on glass, whether as a beginner or as a more experienced practitioner. It is worth remembering, unfired gilding and painting on glass is inherently unstable. Even if you do everything right, things can go wrong. I have given some tips and addressed some possible problems, set down here in the order in which they might arise during work.

Water gilding

Crawling size

If the size is crawling, which means breaking up into rivulets, first check that the glass is clean. It tends to repel the first application of the size so you need to break the surface tension by brushing hard over the area until the size flows in a continuous pool. Surface tension can be reduced by adding one of the following:

* a small amount of sugar to the size
* some soap, but not detergent, which will have the opposite effect
* a few drops of alcohol or meths

Narrow bands of gold or silver

Narrow strips can be carried out of position by too much size. Let the glue spread and flow out, leaving it as long as possible before laying.

Burnished gold breaking away

Once the leaf is dry and it is time to burnish, you may find some of the leaf will come away from the glass. A common cause is dry glass. If you take too long to lay the leaf after wetting, the size starts to break up and run in rivulets; you may not realise you are laying on to dry glass. Try to remember to wet again just before laying leaf, unless you are laying narrow strips of leaf. Be sure to make the size strong enough or it will not hold the leaf. It is best to follow the recipes exactly.

Dull leaf

Remove all traces of whiting from the cleaning process, as the smallest amount will contaminate the gild. Check the size is very clean. Use distilled or rainwater if necessary.

Trouble with engraving

Difficulty with engraving can have several causes:

* the size is too strong
* a greasy deposit from your hands is interfering
* the gilded surface has been left a long time and the gelatine has hardened

Remedies:

* follow the recipe proportions for making the size
* place paper over the gold where you rest your hand
* very lightly abrade the gild with pumice so it will take the engraving

Achieving a solid-looking gild

Back up or cover solid gilding with chrome yellow, which is close in colour to yellow gold and is an especially strong pigment. For silver use a grey.

Wavy tide marks

If these appear along the bottom section of a panel, it might be because the size has travelled back up the glass without being able to run off before drying. Be sure to place panels to dry on props, not directly on the ground.

Painting

Backing up, or covering, leaf

Using a palette knife, decant the paint you need on to a palette from the bottle, tin or can. This will keep the main supply uncontaminated.

Closing paint cans

Sign-writers' paint dries fast, not just on the glass but also in the tin. Keep them closed at all times. A layer of plastic cling film, known also as 'saran wrap', placed over the paint under the lid, helps to prevent it from skinning over. Place the tin on the floor and carefully stand on it to close the lid. Sometimes cans are stored upside down.

Removing dried paint

On occasion it is necessary to remove a layer. It is tricky but it can be done and with care the gilding can be preserved. Let the solvents do their work. Apply the solvent, let it sit and mop it up gently with paper towel. Recoat if necessary. Abrasion will remove leaf, even if the 'right' solvents are used. For dried sign-writers' paint, thinners will not work. Try applying a heavier layer of shellac, such as button polish and let this sit and loosen the paint. Wash it away gently with alcohol or meths. Alcohol or meths alone can be used in successive coats too. Paint stripper will also work, but as a last resort as the residue is difficult to clean up if the gilding is to be preserved. Use thinners for asphaltum.

Removing leaf

Whiting and alcohol or meths, or pumice powder and saliva (good gold-eating enzymes) will clean off the leaf.

Removing dried shellac

Alcohol or meths with fine steel or wire wool.

Safety advice

A workshop needs ventilation but the windows need to be shut to prevent draughts; gold leaf is so light it can easily blow away. Once the gilding is finished and backing up has begun, have at least two windows open to let air pass through. It is important to be aware of every aspect of safety in the studio. Information can be obtained from the website for COSHH, The Control of Substances Hazardous to Health, www.hse.gov.uk/.

Working with glass, areas of damage control are:

* Cuts from glass
* Fumes from solvents
* Skin contact with solvent-based materials
* Handling dry pigments and powders
* Damage limitation in case of fire from solvents
* Disposal of solvents

Cuts from glass

Handling sheets of glass needs great care. It is easy to become complacent and to bang into furniture. Give yourself time above all, and space to move glass around. Dispose of cut glass safely by wrapping well in newspaper and boxing it up in the appropriate containers for the rubbish collectors.

Fumes from solvents

It is sometimes possible to avoid using a hazardous substance by using water-based rather than solvent-based products and by applying with a brush rather than spraying. Regarding alcohol-based products, denatured alcohol, which is almost pure ethanol, is only moderately poisonous and not easily absorbed.

Skin contact with solvent-based materials such as turpentine

Use vinyl or nitrile impermeable, disposable gloves. Wash skin thoroughly with soap and water or use a proprietary skin cleaner. If swallowed, seek medical advice immediately and show the container or label.

Eye Contact: Contact lenses should be removed. Irrigate copiously with clean, fresh water for at least 10 minutes, holding the eyelids apart, and seek medical advice.

Ingestion: If accidentally swallowed obtain medical attention. Do not induce vomiting. In all cases of doubt, or where symptoms persist seek medical attention.

Handling dry pigments and powders

Dry pigments and powders are inhalation hazards and can be ingested easily and bronze or aluminium powders can be explosive. Once they are combined with a liquid they present much less hazard. Using a vacuum cleaner rather than a brush can reduce dust. A good mask is necessary in the studio, with a filter, but masks are designed for different purposes. A dust mask will not act as a vapour mask. The properties of your mask will need to be understood, as will the need for frequent changes of filter.

Damage limitation in case of fire from solvents

Do not use water. Do not breathe in vapour, and avoid contact with skin and eyes.

Disposal of solvents

Do not empty solvent-based liquids into drains. Dispose in accordance with Local Authority Regulations. It is advisable to look up information on hazardous waste disposal in your area.

APPENDIX 1
GLOSSARY

Acrylic paint An emulsion paint using a synthetic medium, acrylic resin, now often used as a quicker-drying substitute for oil paint.

Alcohol This term refers to methylated spirits or denatured alcohol, both of which are ethanols that have additives to make them unfit for human consumption, and rubbing alcohol or 91% isopropyl alcohol, which are ethyl alcohol-isopropyl alcohol mixtures.

Alloy A mixture of different metals. A gold alloy can be anything less than 24 karat, which is pure gold.

Amelieren, (verb); ***Amelierung,*** (noun). A form of reverse engraving on glass. Either powdered metal, painted onto the glass and engraved, or engraved metal leaf, backed with transparent lacquers are used. This in turn is backed with smooth or crinkled metal foil (tin, silver, aluminium etc.) to reflect the light.

Applied art Art which is essentially functional, but which adds aesthetically pleasing decoration to objects like furniture, clocks, textiles, etc..

Artists' oil colours Finely ground pigment suspended in a drying oil, most commonly linseed oil.

Asphaltum A chemically unstable, tar-based pigment which never dries hard and can shrink with age.

Backing up A term to describe the covering and protection of gold on glass, using for example: paint, shellac, leaf, or *découpage*.

Binder The liquid material in which pigment is suspended: linseed oil for oil painting, gum arabic for watercolours. Also known as Medium or Vehicle.

Bitumen see Asphaltum

Broken colour Layers of thin paint broken or distressed to reveal underlying colours.

Burnish (verb), to rub the gilded surface with a soft cloth to smooth and shine it.

Burnish water gilding Gilding carried out with water-based size that can be smoothed and polished to a shine with cotton or cottonwool.

Chinoiserie (French: Chinesesque) Playful imitation of Chinese art and architecture generally associated with the Rococo style in 18th century Europe.

Cold painting, cold colours Unfired decoration with gold leaf and/or painting on glass.

Coloured gesso traditional gesso coloured with the addition of water-based paint or with dry pigment. Used to cover asphaltum.

Cotton (U.S.A.) / cottonwool (U.K.) Soft, fluffy fibre.

Découpage (French: cutting out) The process of cutting out designs of paper and applying them to a surface to make a collage.

Earth colours Pigments such as brown or yellow, which occur naturally are usually metallic oxides. Chemically they are the most stable of all pigments, and are least likely to change in the aging process.

English glass picture A kind of *'faux'* painting on glass whereby a fresh copperplate engraving is placed face down onto glass and varnished overall. Once dry, the paper is wetted and rubbed away, leaving the inked lines fixed to the glass. The lines are in-filled with oil-based paints.

Engraving Removing gold or other metal leaf with tools such as sharpened bone or wood and cut down brushes.

Federal style A style of decoration prevalent in the U.S. from the establishment of the Federal Government in 1789 to c.1830. It was influenced by English and French Neo-Classicism.

Foil Either self-adhesive aluminium for final backing of large panels or thin metal foil used for backing up coloured shellac used for its reflective properties.

Fondi d'oro (Italian: gold ground) A sandwich of two sheets of glass and cut gold foil between. The leaf is applied cold and the whole object is heated in the kiln to fuse all the elements together.

Frieze Architectural term: the part of the entablature between the architrave and the cornice.

Frottage (French: rubbing) Use of crumpled paper or thin plastic to remove wet glaze, revealing the ground colour.

Gelatine size A thin water-based glue made either from capsules or from sheet, as used for cooking.

Gesso Traditionally made with a mix of rabbitskin glue and whiting, this can be used on glass as an opaque, final coat. Acrylic gesso is not suitable for glass.

Gilder's tip Squirrel or badger hair held between sheets of card, for picking up and handling precious leaf.

Gilding The application of a layer of precious metal to glass, wood or other surfaces.

Glair Beaten egg white, used for gluing gold or silver to a surface; a medieval recipe.

Glaze A transparent layer of paint applied over another layer, or over a ground of a different colour in order to modify it.

Glaze medium A viscous material used to modify and extend paint.

Gold engraving Reverse engraved gilding on glass, usually backed with oil-based paint.

Gouache Opaque watercolours with a filler of some form of opaque white (such as clay or barite) giving a typical chalky look.

Gridding Making a grid on paper or directly on the front side of the glass, for use as guidelines for gilding whole leaves.

Grisaille (French: grey tones) painting in grey or greyish monochrome, sometimes heightened with gold.

Japan driers An oil drying agent that can be mixed with oil-based paints to speed up drying.

Karat The term by which the purity of gold is measured.

Lacquer Translucent layers of alcohol or oil-based colour backed with foil.

Marble to render marble or precious stone in paint.

Metal flux brush From the stained glass trade, cut down and used to abrade gold and silver for shading.

Medallion A painting or engraving set in a circular frame.

Medium see Binder, Vehicle

Meths Abbreviation for methylated spirits.

Monochrome A single colour.

Mop Soft squirrel brush for water gilding and for shellac.

Mordant The adhesive used by gilders to secure gold leaf to its substrate, such as paper, wood or paint.

Oxidise The combining of oxygen with metal to cause discoloration.

Patent leaf The term for transfer leaf used in the U.S.A.

Pigment The colouring agent in paint or dye, isolated in dry form usually as a powder.

Reverse engraving see Engraving

Reverse gilding and painting on glass Any non-fired decoration, using metal leaf and paint, applied to the back of glass and viewed from the front.

Schlag (German: beat) A term for Dutch metal, or composition leaf, which is imitation gold leaf.

Scumbling The uneven working of a thin layer of paint over another of a different colour, showing the under layer. It gives a veiled or broken effect.

Singerie A style of decorative painting depicting monkeys acting as humans, popular amongst French artists of the early 18th century.

Size A weak solution of glue used to adhere leaf to glass, whether water or oil-based.

Skewings Scraps of gold collected from the burnished gild.

Steel wool, known as wire wool Soft steel filaments formed to make a scouring pad for cleaning glass.

Striping Applying painted lines with fine brushes, known as 'writers'.

Surface gilding Oil gilding on a surface such as wood or stone.

Tempera An emulsion used as a medium for pigment, traditionally mixed with whole egg or egg yolk.

Thinners Solvents for oil-based paints and varnishes, such as mineral spirits.

Transfer leaf Leaf attached lightly to a tissue paper backing, used mainly for exterior work.

Trompe-l'oeil (French: deceives the eye) Painting which persuades the onlooker that he is seeing actual 3-D objects.

Universal tint A tint or stain for colouring material, soluble in water, alcohol or thinners.

Varnish Resin dissolved in a medium and used either as a protective coating (which can be tinted), or sometimes as a vehicle for pigment, forming a paint.

Verre églomisé (French: glomyised glass) The term has been used since Jean-Baptiste Glomy, 1711–1786, first decorated glass with gold leaf and black paint to frame prints and embroideries. The term, first used in 1852, has since been applied to almost any kind of cold or unfired decoration on the underside of glass, with or without the use of metal leaf. In this publication, the term 'gold engraving' is preferred. For full discussions of the term, see 'Terminology' in chapter 1, pages 1–2 and 16th–17th century in Italy, chapter 3, pages 15–17.

Vitreous Of the nature of glass.

Wash A thin layer of paint, as in water colour.

Whiting Calcium carbonate, as used in the making of gesso.

Zwischengoldglas (German: glass with gold between) Refers to the beakers made in 18th-century Bohemia whereby two clear glass vessels sandwich gold engraving. The process is similar to *fondi d'oro* but uses thinner, engraved gold leaf.

APPENDIX 2
SUPPLIERS OF MATERIALS

Suppliers and materials as described in the book are correct at the time of writing and are subject to change. Try keyword searches on the Internet if you are having difficulty finding materials.

U.K.

DIAMOND PADS

B and H Services
Pilton Place
Cardiff CF14 3DS
Tel: +44 (0)2920 214252
www.bandhservices.co.uk

PIGMENTS, PAINTS, BRUSHES AND
GILDING MATERIALS (alphabetical)

A.S. Handover
Unit 8, Leeds Place
Tollington Park
London N4 3RF
Tel: +44 (0)20 7272 9624
www.handover.co.uk

Bucks Gold Leaf Supplies
1 Chestnut Close
Chalfont St Peter
Gerrards Cross
Buckinghamshire SL9 0AE
Tel: +44 (0)1494 372999
www.bucksgoldleaf.co.uk

Gold Leaf Supplies
Unit C, Ogmore Court,
Abergarw Trading Estate,
Brynmenyn,
Bridgend.
CF32 9LW
Tel: +44 (0)1656 720 566
www.goldleafsupplies.co.uk

L. Cornelissen & Son Ltd.
105 Great Russell St.
London WC1B 3RY
Tel: +44 (0)20 7636 1045
www.cornelissen.com

Stuart R. Stevenson
68 Clerkenwell Road
London EC1M 5QA
Tel: +44 (0)20 7253 1693
www.stuartstevenson.co.uk

W. Habberley Meadows Ltd.
5 Saxon Way
Chelmsley Wood
Birmingham B37 5AY
Tel: 44 (0)121 770 0103
www.habberleymeadows.co.uk

Wrights of Lymm Ltd.
Warrington Lane
Lymm
Cheshire WA13 0SA
Tel: +44 (0)1925 752226
www.stonehouses.co.uk

U.S.A.

WHITING, GILDING MATERIALS,
PIGMENTS, PAINT

Sepp Leaf Products Inc.
381 Park Ave. South
New York, N.Y. 10016
Tel: +00 (212) 683 2840
www.seppleaf.com

Pearl Art & Craft
308 Canal Street
New York, N.Y. 10013-2521
Tel : +00 (212) 431-7932
www.pearlpaint.com

Kremer Pigments
228 Elizabeth St.
New York, N.Y. 10012
Tel: +00 (212) 219 2394
www.kremer-pigmente.de/en

LOS ANGELES
Easy Leaf Products
6001 Santa Monica Blvd.
Los Angeles, CA 90038
Tel: +00 (800) 569–5323
www.genuinemetal.easyleaf.com

APPENDIX 3
BIBLIOGRAPHY

Bieling, G.P.A. 1791, *Anweisung, wie Silhouetten auf Goldgrund hinter Glas zu verfertigen sind*, Nuremberg.

Binnington, F. October, 1989, 'Decorative Draughtsmanship', *Antique Dealer and Collectors Guide*, U.K.

Bornitius, J. 1625, *Traktatus Politicus De rerum sufficientia in republica et civitate procuranda*. Frankfurt.

Brannt, W.T. 1902, *The Painter, Gilder, and Varnisher's Companion*. 27. ed., Henry Carey Baird & Co., Philadelphia.

Bretz, S. 'Maltechnik und Glastechnik in der Hinterglasmalerei 1600 bis 1650', in: *Farbige Kostbarkeiten aus Glas, Kabinettstücke der Zürcher Hinterglasmalerei 1600-1650,* eds. H. Lanz & L. Seelig, Bayerisches Nationalmuseum, Schweizerisches Landesmuseum, Germany, pp. 181–210.

Bretz, S. and Davison, S. 2003, 'Information on the history, technology, deterioration and restoration of reverse paintings on glass', *Conservation and Restoration of Glass,* First edn, Butterworth-Heinemann, Oxford, U.K.

Bretz, S. and Ryser, F. 2000, 'Kleines Handbuch der Hinterglasmalerei. (Petit manuel de la peinture sous verre)', in: *Glanzlichter. Die Kunst der Hinterglasmalerei.* Ausst. Kat. 289–315 edn, Musée Suisse du Vitrail Romont, Museum in der Burg Zug, Switzerland.

Brill, R.H., Aiken, C.A., Novick, David T., Errett, Raymond F. 1980, 'Conservation Problems of , Part 1: Examination and Analyses', in: *Journal of Glass Studies,* Vol. 22, p. 20.

Cennini, C. 1933, 1960, *The Craftsman's Handbook 'Il Libro dell Arte',* 2nd edn, Dover Publications Inc., U.S.A.

Cröker, J.M. 1736 *Der Wohlanführende Mahler,* Jena (reprint Mittenwald 1982).

Dalton, O.M. 1901, 'The Gilded Glasses of the Catacombs', in: *The Archeological Journal,* Vol. 8, pp. 225–253.

Dammert, U. 1993, *Hinterglasmalerei: Europa, China, Indien. Die Sammlung Udo Dammert.* Prestel-Verlag, Munich, Schloßmuseum Murnau, Germany.

Doerner, M. 1984, *The Materials of the Artist,* Harcourt Brace Jovanovich, San Diego, New York, London.

de Mayerne, T.T. 1620, 'Pictoria Sculptoria et Quae Subalternarum Atrium', in: Berger, E.1901, *Quellen für Maltechnik während der Renaissance und deren Folgezeit,* Munich (reprint 1993).

Drahotová, O. 1983, *European Glass,* Peerage Books, London, Boston.

Düchting, H. 2001, *Kandinsky,* Barnes and Noble, U.S.A.

Eden, F.S. June,1932, 'Verre Eglomisé', in : *The Connoisseur,* Vol. 89, pp. 393–396.

Elskus, A. 1982, *The Art of Painting on Glass, Techniques and Designs for Stained Glass*, Charles Scribner's Sons, New York, U.S.A. Obtainable from, http://stainedglass.org/?page_id=440.

Eswarin, R. 1979, 'Terminology of Verre Eglomisé', in: *Journal of Glass Studies,* Vol. 21, pp. 98–101.

Eswarin, R. 1982, 'Reverse Painting on Glass', in: *Glass Circle News,* no. 4, pp. 46–63.

Eswarin, R. 1992, *Reverse Paintings on Glass: The Ryser Collection,* Corning Museum of Glass, New York, U.S.A.

Exhibition Catalogue, 2000, *Glanzlichter, Die Kunst der Hinterglasmalerei,* Hrsg. Schweizerisches Forschungszentrum zur Glasmalerei Romont; Musée Suisse du Vitrail Romont; Museum in der Burg Zug, Switzerland.

Gottsegen, M.G. 2006, *The Painter's Handbook,* Watson-Guptill Publications.

Gudenrath, W. 2006, 'Enameled Glass Vessels, 1425 BCE-1800: The Decorating Process', in: *Journal of Glass Studies,* Vol. 48, pp. 23–70.

Guth, P. 1957, 'Toute la vérité sur le verre églomisé', in: *Connaissance des Arts,* Vol. 2, no. 66, pp. 28–33.

Hahn, O., Bretz, S., Hagnau, C., Ranz, H-J., Wolff, T., December, 2009, 'Pigments, Dyes And Black Enamel – the colourants of reverse paintings on glass', in: *Archaeological and Anthropological Sciences, No. 4,* pp. 263–271.

Honey, W.B. September, 1933, 'Gold Engraving Under Glass', in: *The Connoisseur,* Vol. 92, pp. 372–381.

Honey, W.B. (ed.) 1949, *Many Occasions: Essays Towards the Appreciation of Several Arts,* Faber and Faber, London U.K.

Honey, W.B. 1946, *Glass, A Handbook and Guide to the Museum Collection,* Victoria and Albert Museum, London.

Jolidon, Y. 1999, 'Die Zürcher Hinterglasmalerei in der ersten Hälfte des 17. Jahrhunderts' in: *Farbige Kostbarkeiten aus Glas, Kabinettstücke der Zürcher Hinterglasmalerei 1600-1650',* eds. H. Lanz & L. Seelig, Bayerisches Nationalmuseum, Schweizerisches Landesmuseum, Germany, p. 49.

Kelly, A.A. 1910, *The Expert Sign Painter,* Press of The Horace F. Temple Printing and Stationery Co., U.S.A.

Klesse, B., Mayr, H. 1987, *European Glass from 1500-1800,* Kremayr and Scheriau, Vienna.

Knaipp, F. 1988, *Hinterglaskünste,* Callwey, Germany.

Kunckel, J. 1689, *Ars vitraria oder Vollkommene Glasmacher-Kunst. 2.* Reprint, Georg Olms Verlag, Hildesheim, Zurich, New York 1992.

Lanz, H. & Seelig, L. (eds.) 1999, *Farbige Kostbarkeiten aus Glas, Kabinettstücke der Zürcher Hinterglasmalerei 1600-1650,* First edn, Ausst. Kat. Bayerisches Nationalmuseum, Munich; Schweizerisches Landesmuseum, Zurich, Switzerland.

Leblanc, R.J. 1980, *Gold Leaf Techniques,* The Signs of the Times Pub. Co., Ohio, U.S.A.

Lucie-Smith, E. 1984, *The Thames and Hudson Dictionary of Art Terms*, London.

Mactaggart, P. and A. 1984, *Practical Gilding,* Mac & Me Ltd.

Mayer, R. 1981, *The Artist's Handbook of Materials and Techniques,* 4th edn, Faber and Faber, London, Boston.

Merian, M. 1641, translation of Thomas Garzoni *Piazza Universale,* Frankfurt.

Merrifield, M.P. 1967, *Medieval and Renaissance Treatises on the Arts of Painting,* Dover Publications Inc.

Mitchell, F.S. 1915, *Practical Gilding, Bronzing, Lacquering and Glass Embossing,* The Trade Papers Publishing Co. Ltd, London.

Neri, A., trans. Merrett, C. 2001, *The Art of Glass,* Society of Glass Technology.

Newton, R. & Davison, S. 1997, *Conservation of Glass,* paperback edn., Butterworth-Heinemann, London, Boston.

Ritz, G.M. 1972, *Hinterglasmalerei – Geschichte, Erscheinung, Technik,* Munich.

Ritz, G. M. 1964/65, 'Die Bürgerliche-Handwerkliche Hinterglasmalerei des 18. Jh'. in: *Augsburg, Bayerisches Jahrbuch für Volkskunde,* Munich.

Rydlová, E. 2007, 'Zwischengoldgläser from the Museum of Decorative Arts in Prague', in: *Journal of Glass Studies,* Vol. 49, p. 103.

Ryser, F. 1991, *Verzauberte Bilder,* First edn, Klinkhardt & Biermann, Germany.

Ryser, F. & Salmen, B. 1995, *Amalierte Stuck uff Glas/Hinder Glas gemalte Historien und Gemäld. Hinterglaskunst von der Antike bis zur Neuzeit,* Schloßmuseum Murnau, Germany.

Scheurl, Dr C. 1908, 'Account Book from 1532, Nuremberg' in: *Anzeiger des Germanischen Nationalmuseums,* Gazette of German Nationalmuseum.

Schiffer, H. F. 1983, *The Mirror Book,* Schiffer Publishing.

Smith, K. H. 1998, *Gold Leaf Techniques,* ST Media Group International Inc., Cincinnati, U.S.A.

Stahl, E.J. 1915, Dekorative Glasmalerei, *Unterglasmalerei und Malen auf Glas*, U. Hartlebens Verlag, Vienna, Leipzig.

Steiner, W. 2004, *Hinterglas und Kupferstich: Hinterglasgemälde und ihre Vorlagen 1550-1850; Reverse Paintings on Glass*, Hirmer Verlag, Germany.

Strasser, R.v. & Spiegl, W. 1989, *Dekoriertes Glas, Renaissance bis Biedermeie,* Klinkhardt & Biermann.

Theophilus 1979*, On Divers Arts, The Foremost Medieval Treatise on Painting, G;assmaking and Metalwork.* Translated from the Latin with introductions and notes by John G. Hawthorne and Cyril Stanley Smith, Dover Publications, New York.

Von Grimmelshausen H.J.C. 1668, *The Adventuresome Simplicius Simplicissimus* http://en.wikipedia.org/wiki/Hans_Jakob_ Christoffel_von_Grimmelshausen.

von Saldern, A. 1976, 'Zwischengoldgläser mit Marmorierter Lackbemalung', from *Germanisches Nationalmuseum,* Nuremberg www.glasforschung.info/pageone/pdf/ zwigo_2.pdf.

Wessels, E. 1913, *Die Hinterglasmalerei. Anleitung zur Herstellung von Malereien hinter und unter Glas sowie Glasmalerei-Imitationen, Glas-Vergoldung und dergl,* Neff Verlag, Esslingen.

Whitehouse, D. 2001, *Roman Glass in the Corning Museum of Glass,* Volume 1, The Corning Museum of Glass, New York.

APPENDIX 4
PICTURE CREDITS

Cover *Front*, Frances Federer
Back, Misha Bruk
Portrait of the author, Rhian Ap Gruffydd

Chapter 1
1 Bruce Jackson
2 'Black Cat Studio' San Rafael, California.

Chapter 2
1 Ceramics Collection, Victoria and Albert
   Museum, London
2 Frances Federer
3 Raymond Fortt Studios
4, 5 Frances Federer
6 Collection Steiner
7 Mieke Groot
8 Apter-Fredericks Ltd
9 Frances Federer
10 Dave Smith
11 Rob Popper
12 Jonathon Rose
13 Ester Segarra

Chapter 3
Collection Wolfgang Steiner

Chapter 4
1 Frances Federer
2 Ray Main
3 Bruce Jackson
4 Ken Kast

Chapter 5
1, 3 Frances Federer
2 Peter Binnington, for Anouska Hempel

Chapter 6
1–5, 7, 12, 13, 19 , 24, 26, 28, 35, Misha Bruk
6, 8–11,14–18, 20–23, 25, 27, 29–34, 36–38 Stefan
   Majka
39 Rhian Ap Gruffydd

Chapter 7
1–5,9–21, Misha Bruk
6 Peter Binnington
7, 8, 22, 23, 25, 26, 27, 28, 30, 31, 32 Frances
   Federer
24 Collection Wolfgang Steiner
29 By kind permission of Kunstgewerbemuseum,
   Berlin, Germany

APPENDIX 5
NOTES

For the interested reader who wishes to pursue the details in this book further, sources of quotations and extended details of recipes can be found on the page numbers below relating to the books in the Bibliography.

1 Eswarin, 1991, p. 10
2 Eden, 1932, pp. 393–396
3 Honey, 1933, pp. 372–381
4 Guth, 1957, pp. 28–33
5 Guth, 1957, pp. 28–33
6 Eswarin, 1979, pp. 98–101
7 Ryser, 1991, pp. 289–292; Corning 1992, pp. 38–40
8 Romont/Zug, 2000, pp. 290, 302–303, figs.19–22
9 Cennini, 1960, p. 112
10 Steiner, 2004 p. 7
11 Ryser, 1991, pp. 138–150
12 Schiffer, 1983, p. 63, fig. 125
13 Jean Bérain, 1638–1711
14 Ritz, 1972, p. 21
15 Steiner, 2004, fig. 96
16 Ryser, 1991, pp. 223–233
17 Eswarin, 1991, figs. 71–75, pp. 109–114
18 Romont/Zug, 2000, p. 182, fig.10; Orchard *et al*, 1978, pp. 1–21
19 See for examples, Whitehouse, 2001, p. 239; Ryser, 1991, pp. 34, 306, fig. 23; Glanzlichter, 2000, p. 56, cat. no.24, fig. 24
20 Theophilus,1979, pp. 59–60
21 Berger, 1912, p. 13
22 Merrifield, 1967, chap. 269 p. 526
23 Kunckel, 1689, p. 345
24 See for example in Ryser, 1991, pp. 44,307, fig.42; Corning, 1992, p. 12, fig. 5
25 Cennini, 1933, pp.112–114
26 For example see in Ryser, 1991, pp. 84, 320–321, fig. 99, p. 94
27 Merrifield 1967, p. 620, no. 339
28 Hahn *et al.* 2009, p .266
29 Scheurl, 1908, p .107
30 For example see in Ryser, 1991, pp. 81, 318, fig.86–88, p. 90
31 Merian, 1641, p. 612
32 Kunckel, 1689, p. 347
33 Kunckel, 1689, pp. 342–343, 346
34 Kunckel, 1689, p. 345, no. XXI.
35 Bornitius, 1625, p. 169
36 de Mayerne, in Berger, 1901, no. 267, p. 302
37 Ryser, 1991, pp. 151
38 Cröker, 1736, p. 404
39 Bieling, 1791, p. 20
40 Ritz, 1964/65, p. 66
41 Brannt, 1902, pp. 267, 276
42 Wessels, 1913, pp. 65, 67

APPENDIX 6
ACKNOWLEDGEMENTS

I would like to thank *all* the family, especially Stefan, for tolerating this extensive and long drawn out process.

Jane Dorner deserves particular thanks for her untiring, solid and professional input that, I can confidently say, made this book possible.

Simone Bretz and Wolfgang Steiner deserve an enormous 'thank you' for contributions in words and pictures that make the book a unique publication. Other contributors to whom I am very grateful and whose contributions have been very important are: Peter Binnington, long time friend and associate; Jane Richardson Mack, Bruce Jackson, Eva Lee and Dave Smith. Also, Roderick Thomson, for his loyal friendship and excellent contacts, Sue Govani for her generosity and enterprising instincts and numerous friends and students who have chipped in with tips of all kinds and with lots of encouragement for this ambitious enterprise.

APPENDIX 7
NOTES ON CONTRIBUTORS

Simone Bretz is a private conservator based in Bavaria, Germany. Since 1985 she has specialized in the conservation and restoration of reverse paintings on glass and published widely on the subject. She has worked for a number of major museums and private collections in Europe and the United States and contributed her expertise to research projects both in Germany and abroad (see www.bretz-hinterglas.com).

William Gudenrath is a glassblower, scholar, teacher and resident advisor of The Studio of The Corning Museum of Glass. He is recognised internationally as one of the foremost authorities on glassmaking techniques from the ancient world to the 18th century. In addition to his numerous contributions in books, DVDs and videos on many aspects of glass history, Mr Gudenrath maintains an artistic practice and his glass is sold in stores and galleries nationwide.

Wolfgang Steiner
Born in 1938 and living in Germany, since 1997 Wolfgang Steiner has been committed to his occupation as a researcher of *Hinterglasmalerei*. As well as caring for a collection he is an exhibition curator and the author of several important publications. He is the initiator of the annual, 2-day *Hinterglaskunst* conference that takes place at different locations around Germany.

✒ INDEX ✒